THE P̶R̶O̶M̶I̶S̶E̶

and

AT THE POINT OF NEED

Two plays by Paul Unwin

‖ SAMUEL FRENCH ‖

photocopying, recording, videotaping, or otherwise, without the prior written permission of the publisher. No one shall share this title, or part of this title, to any social media or file hosting websites.

The moral right of Paul Unwin to be identified as author of this work has been asserted in accordance with Section 77 of the Copyright, Designs and Patents Act 1988.

USE OF COPYRIGHTED MUSIC

A licence issued by Concord Theatricals to perform this play does not include permission to use the incidental music specified in this publication. In the United Kingdom: Where the place of performance is already licensed by the PERFORMING RIGHT SOCIETY (PRS) a return of the music used must be made to them. If the place of performance is not so licensed then application should be made to PRS for Music (www.prsformusic.com). A separate and additional licence from PHONOGRAPHIC PERFORMANCE LTD (www.ppluk.com) may be needed whenever commercial recordings are used. Outside the United Kingdom: Please contact the appropriate music licensing authority in your territory for the rights to any incidental music.

USE OF COPYRIGHTED THIRD-PARTY MATERIALS

Licensees are solely responsible for obtaining formal written permission from copyright owners to use copyrighted third-party materials (e.g., artworks, logos) in the performance of this play and are strongly cautioned to do so. If no such permission is obtained by the licensee, then the licensee must use only original materials that the licensee owns and controls. Licensees are solely responsible and liable for clearances of all third-party copyrighted materials, and shall indemnify the copyright owners of the play(s) and their licensing agent, Concord Theatricals Ltd., against any costs, expenses, losses and liabilities arising from the use of such copyrighted third-party materials by licensees.

IMPORTANT BILLING AND CREDIT REQUIREMENTS

If you have obtained performance rights to this title, please refer to your licensing agreement for important billing and credit requirements.

NOTE

This edition reflects a rehearsal draft of the script and may differ from the final production.

THE PROMISE

THE PROMISE was originally produced by Chichester Festival Theatre, and was first performed at the Minerva Theatre on 19 July 2024. The cast and creative team were as follows:

ELLEN WILKINSON . . . . Clare Burt
CLEMENT ATTLEE . . . . Andrew Woodall
VIOLET ATTLEE . . . . Suzanne Burden
HERBERT MORRISON . . . . Reece Dinsdale
ERNIE BEVIN . . . . Clive Wood
NYE BEVAN . . . . Richard Harrington
JENNIE LEE . . . . Allison McKenzie
HUGH DALTON . . . . Miles Richardson
RICHARD STAFFORD CRIPPS . . . . Peter Hamilton Dyer
LORD MORAN (CHARLIE WILSON) . . . . David Robb
WINSTON CHURCHILL . . . . Martyn Ellis
JOAN VINCENT . . . . Felixe Forde
PHOTOGRAPHER/THOMAS MERRIMAN . . . . Majid Mehdizadeh-Valoujerdy

Writer. . . . . Paul Unwin
Director . . . . Jonathan Kent
Set Designer . . . . Joanna Parker
Costume Designer & Supervisor . . . . Deborah Andrews
Lighting and Video Designer. . . . . Peter Mumford
Composer . . . . Gary Yershon
Sound Designer . . . . Christopher Shutt
Casting Director. . . . . Annelie Powell CDG
Dramaturg. . . . . Harry Mackrill
Associate Set Designer . . . . Christophe Eynde
Assistant Director . . . . Sydney Stevenson
Production Manager . . . . Matt Ledbury
Props Supervisor . . . . Fahmida Bakht
Company Stage Manager . . . . Alison Rankin
Deputy Stage Manager . . . . Caitlin Shay
Assistant Stage Manager . . . . Emily Humphrys

chichester festival theatre

Chichester Festival Theatre creates inspiring experiences that bring people together – on and off the stage. Creativity is at the heart of everything we do, and we aim to light a spark in everyone who experiences our work – locally, regionally, nationally and internationally.

As one of the UK's flagship theatres, we are renowned for the exceptionally high standard of our productions and our industry-leading work with the community and young people. Situated in a cathedral city in West Sussex between the South Downs and the sea, the Festival Theatre's bold thrust stage design makes it one of England's most striking playhouses – equally suited to epic drama and musicals. The studio theatre, the Minerva, is particularly noted for premieres of new work alongside intimate revivals.

The annual summer Festival season runs from April to October, during which all productions are originated at Chichester. Countless productions which started life at CFT have transferred to the West End or toured nationally and internationally over the past six decades, from musicals to significant new plays and classic revivals. London transfers include Susan Stroman's production of *Crazy for You*, Steven Moffat's *The Unfriend*, *South Pacific*, *Singin' in the Rain*, Laura Wade's *The Watsons*, *Caroline, or Change* (also on Broadway), Ian McKellen in *King Lear* (also broadcast to cinemas internationally by NT Live) and James Graham's *Quiz*. Our co-production with the National Theatre of Alecky Blythe's *Our Generation* is available to stream on NT At Home.

Year-round programming continues through the winter with the Theatre presenting high-class touring drama, music and comedy, as well as a traditional Christmas show by the renowned Chichester Festival Youth Theatre.

Our Learning, Education and Participation (LEAP) department works with people of all ages and abilities, offering a pioneering range of initiatives that inspire and delight all those who take part.

To read more about who we are and what we do, visit cft.org.uk.

Chair . . . . Mark Foster
Artistic Director . . . . Justin Audibert
Executive Director . . . . Kathy Bourne
Theatre Manager. . . . . Janet Bakose
Technical Director. . . . . Sam Garner-Gibbons
Director of Learning, Education and Participation . . . . Dale Rooks
Director of Marketing and Communications. . . . . Luke Shires

CAST

SUZANNE BURDEN | Violet Attlee

Previously at Chichester: Maria in *Twelfth Night* (Festival Theatre); Lady Macduff in *Macbeth*, Lydia Cruttwell in *In Praise of Love*, Beth in *Three Women and a Piano Tuner* (Minerva Theatre).

Theatre includes Herodius in *Salome, The Comedy of Errors, Solstice, The Winter's Tale* (tour), *Les Liaisons Dangereuses* (also West End/Broadway) and *Postcards from America*, all Royal Shakespeare Company; Queen Elizabeth I in *Shakespeare in Love* (Noël Coward Theatre); Hippolyta in *'Tis Pity She's a Whore* (Cheek by Jowl); Mrs Hudetz in *Judgement Day, King Lear, The Possibilities, When We Dead Awaken* (Almeida); Mrs Alving in *Ghosts* (Arcola); Olivia in *The Chalk Garden* (Donmar Warehouse); *Battle Royal, The Recruiting Officer, The White Chameleon, Hedda Gabler, The Voysey Inheritance, The Shaughraun, Piano* (National Theatre); *By Many Wounds* (Hampstead Theatre); *Heartbreak House* (Edinburgh Royal Lyceum); *As You Like It* (Royal Exchange Theatre).

Television includes *Strike* series 3, 4 & 5, *Black Mirror 5, Fresh Meat, Midsomer Murders, Campion, Poirot, Fear Stress and Anger, Life Begins, Absolute Power, Armadillo, Microsoap, The Vet, A Mind to Murder, Between the Lines, Soldier Soldier, You Me and It, 'Tis Pity She's a Whore, Secret Orchards, The Cherry Orchard, Troilus and Cressida, An Office Romance, Sharma and Beyond, Love in a Cold Climate, Bleak House, Hard Travelling, The Rivals*.

Radio includes *Charles Paris: So Much Blood, Waking the Dead, The Charles Paris Mystery*.

Films include *Joy, Gertler, The Devotee, Very Like a Whale, Strapless*.

Trained at RADA.

CLARE BURT | Ellen Wilkinson

Previously at Chichester: Ada Harris in *Flowers for Mrs Harris* (Festival Theatre), Yvonne in *This is My Family* (Minerva Theatre).

Theatre includes *Stephen Sondheim's Old Friends* (Gielgud Theatre); Ada in *Flowers for Mrs Harris* (winner of the UK Theatre Award 2016), Yvonne in *This is My Family* (Sheffield Crucible); *London Road, The Miracle, DNA, Babygirl, Coram Boy, Sunday in the Park with George* (National Theatre); *The American Clock* (Old Vic); Joan Littlewood in *Miss Littlewood* (RSC); *Big Fish* (The Other Palace); *The Divide* (Edinburgh Festival/Old Vic); *Sunspots* (Hampstead Theatre); *Game* (Almeida Theatre); *A Streetcar Named Desire, Vernon God Little* (Young Vic); *Into the Woods, Company, Nine* (Donmar Warehouse); *Now You Know* (Metropolitan Room New York/Pizza on the Park); *The Hired Man* (Astoria Theatre); *Passion* (Bridewell).

Television includes *Sexy Beast, The Couple Next Door, Friday Night Dinner, The Children Next Door, Top Boy, Alice & Jack, Passenger, The Long Shadow, Tina and Bobby, Call the Midwife, Holby City, The Salisbury Poisonings, Cuffs, Criminal Justice, Fair Cop.*

Films include *London Road, Broken, X+Y, The Levelling.*

REECE DINSDALE | Herbert Morrison

Theatre includes Solness in *(The Fall of) The Master Builder,* title role in *Richard III,* Alan Bennett in *Untold Stories,* Ross in *Visiting Mr Green,* Vindice in *The Revenger's Tragedy,* Christy in *Playboy of the Western World,* Jack Rover in *Wild Oats* (Leeds Playhouse); George Jones in *The Absence of War* (Headlong); Walter Harrison in *This House,* Rev Tony Ferris in *Racing Demon* (National Theatre); Dr Wangel in *Lady from the Sea,* Posa in *Don Carlos,* Jimmy in *Woundings* (Royal Exchange Theatre); Gary in *Boys Mean Business,* Jim in *Love You Too* (Bush Theatre); Cavaliere in *Mirandolina* (Lyric Theatre); Craig in *Observe the Sons of Ulster Marching Towards the Somme,* Tony in *A Going Concern, Morning and Evening* (Hampstead); Martin in *Old Year's Eve* (RSC); Berenger in *Rhinoceros* (Nuffield); Terry in *Red Saturday* (Paines Plough/Royal Court); Pascal in *Beethoven's Tenth* (Vaudeville).

Television includes *Threads, Silent Witness, Life on Mars, Conviction, Spooks, Home to Roost, Ahead of the Class, The Storyteller, Take Me Home, The Attractions, Moving On, Catherine the Great, The Investigation, Coppers, In Deep, Murder in Mind, Thief Takers, Midnight Man, Love Lies Bleeding, Born and Bred, Haggard, Taggart, Waterloo Road, Dalziel and Pascoe, The Chase, Lovejoy, Bliss, Full Stretch, Bergerac, Robin of Sherwood, Glamour Night, Out on the Floor, Partners in Crime, The Secret Adversary, Knife Edge, Coronation Street, Emmerdale.*

As a director: *Eighteen, Scratch, Man of Steel, Madge, Lost,* "Beaten" for *Moving On, Coronation Street, Emmerdale.*

Radio: numerous plays and series.

Films include *ID* (Special Jury Prize – Geneva Film Festival), *Hamlet, A Private Function, Winter Flight, The Knife That Killed Me, Rabbit on the Moon, Romance and Rejection.*

As a writer: *Imaginary Friend.*

Trained at Guildhall School of Music and Drama.

PETER HAMILTON DYER | Richard Stafford Cripps

Previously at Chichester: *Mansfield Park* (Festival Theatre).

Theatre includes *#We Are Arrested, A Midsummer Night's Dream, Dream 16: A Play for the Nation, Epicoene* (RSC); *Twelfth Night, Richard III* (Shakespeare's Globe/West End/Broadway); *King Lear* (Shakespeare's Globe/Tokyo); *The Comedy of Errors, The Tempest, Henry VIII, All's Well That Ends Well, Antony and Cleopatra, The Changeling, The Broken Heart, Anne Boleyn, Gabriel, The Frontline, Holding Fire!, The Golden Ass* (Shakespeare's Globe); *Romeo and Juliet* (Regent's Park); *The Last King of Scotland* (Sheffield); *One Flew Over the Cuckoo's Nest* (Nimax UK tour); *The Bacchae* (Shared Experience); *Richard II, The Moonstone* (Royal Exchange Theatre Manchester); *Mrs Orwell* (Southwark Playhouse); *The Caretaker, David Copperfield* (Dundee Rep); *The Norman Conquests* (Basingstoke); *Saint Joan* (Birmingham Rep); *Comfort Me With Apples* (Hampstead Theatre); *Miss Julie* (Southampton).

Television includes *Wolf Hall: The Mirror and the Light, The Confessions of Frannie Langton, The Nest, Genius: Einstein, Downton Abbey, Wolf Hall, Silk, Doctor Who, Exterminate all the Brutes, Upstart Crow, EastEnders, Babs, Doctors, The Bill, Silent Witness, Holby City, Waking the Dead, The Plot Against Harold Wilson, The Curse of Steptoe.*

Radio includes *The Sisters, The Venice Conundrum, My Friend: Marie Antoinette, BBC Radio Rep, R4 Book of The Week: Then They Came For Me, Scribblers, Bretton Woods, Pilgrim, The Colour of Milk, Brother Dusty Feet, Songs and Lamentations, The Cruel Sea, Mrs Dalloway, Ulysses, Twelfth Night, Titanic, Black Dirt, The House in the Trees, Caligari, Waiting for the Boatman, Bournewood, The Day Dad Stole A Bus, The Tempest, Caligari, The Grudge, The British Club, Red and Blue, The Warrah, Trueman and Riley, Blue Flu, The Lifeblood.*

MARTYN ELLIS | Winston Churchill

Previously at Chichester: Jimmy in *Sing Yer Heart Out for the Lads* (Spiegeltent).

Theatre includes Marcus Lycus in *A Funny Thing Happened on the Way to the Forum* (Lido Paris); Alfred P. Doolittle in *My Fair Lady* (Teatro Massimo, Palermo, and Teatro di San Carlo, Naples); Sir Toby Belch in *Twelfth Night* (Young Vic); The Wizard in *Wicked*, Thenardier in *Les Misérables*, Man 2 in *The 39 Steps*, Pumbaa in original London cast of *The Lion King* and Paul McCartney in *Lennon* (West End); Gangster 1 in *Kiss Me, Kate* (Théatre du Chatêlet, Paris); Harry Dangle in original cast of *One Man, Two Guvnors* (National Theatre, West End and Broadway); Alfred P Doolittle in *My Fair Lady* and Dromio of Ephesus in *The Boys from Syracuse* (Sheffield Crucible); Nicely-Nicely Johnson in *Guys and*

Dolls (Piccadilly Theatre, WhatsOnStage Award for Best Supporting Actor in a Musical); Herman Preysing in *Grand Hotel* (Donmar); Mr Biggins in *Moll Flanders* (Lyric Hammersmith); Dafydd in *A Chorus of Disapproval* (Bristol Old Vic).

Television includes *Moonflower Murders, The Playlist, Grime Kids, Renegade Nell, The Witcher, Why Didn't They Ask Evans?, Liaison, It's A Sin, The Accident, The Light, A Confession, Catch 22, The Romanoffs, Decline and Fall, The Last Kingdom, Father Brown, Harley and the Davidsons, The Smoke, Jonathan Strange and Mr Norrell, Agatha Raisin, The Sarah Jane Adventures, The Bobinogs, Fun with Claude, Doctors, The Tudors, Doctors and Nurses, William and Mary, The New Adventures of Robin Hood, Lifeboat, Rockliffe's Babies, Joking Apart, Kavanagh QC.*

Films include *Christmas Eve, A Christmas Carol, Devil's Bridge, Agent Cody Banks: Lost in London, In2Minds.*

Trained at Central School of Speech and Drama.

FELIXE FORDE | Joan Vincent

Theatre includes Juliet in *Playing Shakespeare: Romeo and Juliet* (Shakespeare's Globe); Richmond in *Henry VI: Rebellion*, Bevis in *Henry VI: Wars of the Roses* (RSC); *Pride and Prejudice* (*sort of)* (Bristol Old Vic & UK tour); *The Afflicted* (Edinburgh Fringe Festival); *Petroleuse* (Lyric Hammersmith/Evolution Festival).

Television includes *The Chelsea Detective, Midsomer Murders, Death in Paradise, Doctors.*

Trained at the Royal Conservatoire of Scotland.

RICHARD HARRINGTON | Nye Bevan

Theatre includes Johnny in *Home I'm Darling* (National Theatre/Duke of York's); Aufidius in *Coriolanus* (National Theatre of Wales/RSC); Messenger in *The Persians* (NTW); Cliff in *Look Back in Anger* (Theatre Royal Bath); Steve in *Other Hands*, Art in *Art and Gruff* (Soho Theatre); Ray in *Stone City Blue* (Theatr Clwyd); Gary in *Unprotected Sex*, Brian in *Gas Station Angel* (Royal Court); *House of America* (UK tour/Fiction Factory).

Television includes *Tree On A Hill, McDonald and Dodds, The One That Got Away, Steeltown Murders, Dalgliesh, Consent, The Chelsea Detective, Endeavour, Gangs of London, A Mother's Love, The Crown, Death in Paradise, Father Brown, Inspector George Gently, Requiem, Hinterland, Poldark, Woolfblood, Larkrise to Candleford, Collision, Land Girls, MI High, Missing, New Tricks, 5 Days, HolbyBlue, Sold, Casualty, Rise and Fall of Rome, Bleak House, Dalziel & Pascoe, Hustle, Silent Witness, Spooks, Gunpowder Treason and Plot, Holby City, Rehab, Care, Score.*

Radio includes *Release, Castle of the Hawk, The Aeneid, Words & Music: Innocence, One Horizon, The Kraken Waves, A Child's Christmas in Wales, Antony and Cleopatra, And Quiet Flows the Don, Station Road, Night Must Fall, A Civil War, The Assassin, The Elizabethans, The Great Subterranean Adventure.*

Films include *Havoc, Fisherman's Friends 2, The Most Reluctant Convert, Gwen, The Last Summer, Just Jim, Elfie Hopkins, Burton – The Secret, Daddy's Girl, The Contractor, The All Together, Mathilde, Secret Passage, Joyrider, House of America.*

ALLISON MCKENZIE | Jennie Lee

Previously at Chichester: Isobel in *The Butterfly Lion* (Minerva Theatre).

Theatre includes Steph in *Wilderness* (Hampstead Theatre); Lavinia in *Seven Acts of Mercy*, Hippolyta in *The Two Noble Kinsmen*, Moretta in *The Rover* (RSC); The White Witch in *The Lion the Witch and the Wardrobe* (Birmingham Rep); Lady Macduff/Witch in *Macbeth* (Trafalgar Studios); *Doctor in the House* (UK tour); *The Snow Queen, Hamlet* (Edinburgh Lyceum); Lady Macbeth in *Macbeth* (Nottingham Playhouse/Edinburgh Lyceum); *Witchcraft* (Finborough Theatre); *James and the Giant Peach* (Citizens Theatre); *All My Sons*, Sally Bowles in *Cabaret* (TMA nomination for Best Actress), *Sexual Perversity in Chicago, The Playboy of the Western World* (Dundee Repertory Theatre).

Television includes *Our House, Shetland, Beowulf, Crime, The Victim, Press, Line of Duty, River City, The Athena, Rebus.*

Trained at the Royal Conservatoire of Scotland.

MAJID MEHDIZADEH-VALOUJERDY | Photographer/Thomas Merriman

Theatre includes Phil in *The Shape of Things* (Park Theatre); Himself in *Y'MAM (Young Man's Angry Movements)* (Soho Theatre, Liverpool Everyman & UK tour); title role in *Peter Pan* (Theatre by the Lake); Sebastian in *Twelfth Night* (Liverpool Everyman); Albert Narracott in *War Horse* (New London Theatre); Andrukha Repin in *Galka Motalka* (Royal Exchange Theatre Studio).

Television includes *Testament, Doctor Who, The Girlfriend Experience, Hollyoaks, Doctors.*

Radio includes *Central Intelligence, Convenience Store Woman, In Diamond Square, Love Thy Synth, Indigo Children, Higher: Rebrand Relaunch, Voices Through the Wall.*

Films include *Chosen, Act/Or, The Turing Enigma.*

Majid is Senior Lecturer in Acting for Stage and Screen at the University of East London. Trained at Manchester School of Theatre.

Instagram @majidmvj

MILES RICHARDSON | Hugh Dalton

Theatre includes over 70 plays in the West End and in numerous repertory companies as well as touring at home and aboard; most recently, *The Mousetrap* (St Martin's Theatre); *My Fair Lady* (Frinton Summer Theatre); *Witness for the Prosecution* (County Hall); *Remains of the Day* (Out of Joint tour); *This House* (National Theatre tour). He spent five years at the Royal Shakespeare Company appearing in *Love's Labour's Lost, All's Well That Ends Well, A Midsummer Night's Dream, As You Like It, Volpone, Henry IV Parts 1 & 2, Henry V, Henry VI Parts 1, 2 & 3, Richard III.*

Other credits include *Dear Brutus, The Moment of Truth* (Southwark Playhouse); *Sleuth* (Nottingham Playhouse); *King John* (Rose Theatre); *King Charles III* (Wyndham's Theatre/Broadway); *12 Angry Men* (Garrick Theatre); *Anjin: The Shogun and the English Samurai* (Tokyo & Sadler's Wells); *Macbeth, Death of a Salesman, The Caucasian Chalk Circle* (Newcastle Rep); *Another Country* (Queen's); *Romeo and Juliet* (Ludlow Festival); *Wilfred, A Midsummer Night's Dream, An Inspector Calls, The Contractor* (Birmingham Rep); *Othello* (Theatr Clwyd); *Private Lives* (Theatre Royal York); *Richard II, Richard III, The Three Musketeers* (national tours); *An Evening with Gary Lineker* (Lyric); *The Seagull* (Bromley); *Journey's End* (King's Head); *Charley's Aunt, The Three Musketeers* (Canizzaro Park); *The Picture of Dorian Gray* (Westminster Theatre); *The Invisible Man* (Stratford East/Vaudeville Theatre/Harold Pinter Theatre); *Candida, The Lovers, Playing Sinatra* (New End); *Lulu* (Almeida & Washington DC).

Television includes *Industry, Doctors, The Canterville Ghost, Outlander, Sicknote, The Crown, Genius, Lucan, Jo, Dancing on the Edge, Upstairs Downstairs, Titanic.*

Films include *The Courier, Cranley Gardens, Peterloo, A Quiet Passion.*

Trained at Arts Educational Drama College, winning the Best Actor Award.

DAVID ROBB | Lord Moran (Charlie Wilson)

Previously at Chichester: *Treasure Island, The Taming of the Shrew, The Beggar's Opera* (Festival Theatre).

Theatre includes Michael Mansfield/Ray Bailey in *Value Engineering: Scenes from the Grenfell Enquiry* (Tabernacle Theatre & Birmingham Rep); Sir Anthony Blunt in *Single Spies* (UK tour); Sir Anthony Eden in *The Audience* (Apollo Theatre); Claudius in *Hamlet* (West End & UK tour); Duke of Cornwall in *King Lear* (Almeida Theatre); George in *Same Time Next Year*, Elyot Chase in *Private Lives*, Sir David Lindsay in *Armstrong's Last Goodnight* (Royal Lyceum, Edinburgh); Michael Mansfield in *The Colour of Justice* (NT & UK tour); Lord Goring in *An Ideal Husband* (Old Vic); Michael Heseltine in *Half the Picture* (Tricycle Theatre).

Television includes *Downton Abbey, Wolf Hall, Garrow's Law, Sharpe's Peril, The Roman Mysteries, Rebus, Taggart, Monarch of the Glen, Heartbeat, In the Company of Strangers, Midsomer Murders, The Broker's Man, The Crow Road, Casualty, Highlander, Half the Picture, Takin' Over the Asylum, Strathblair, Up the Garden Path, Parnell and the Englishwoman, The Man Who Lived at The Ritz, Wall of Tyranny, Dreams Lost, Dreams Found, First Among Equals, Off Peak, The Last Days of Pompeii, Le Mort d'Arthur, Hamlet, Dangerous Corner, Ivanhoe, Fanny by Gaslight, The Flame Trees of Thika, The Legend of King Arthur, Forgive Our Foolish Ways, I, Claudius, The Glittering Prizes.*

Films include *Downton Abbey: A New Era, Sacrifice, From Time to Time, Young Victoria, Elizabeth: The Golden Age, The Life and Death of Peter Sellers, The Deceivers, The Four Feathers, Regeneration, Conduct Unbecoming.*

CLIVE WOOD | Ernie Bevin

Theatre includes Marc Antony in *Antony and Cleopatra* (Shakespeare's Globe); Ben in *The Dumb Waiter* (The Print Room); Gloucester in *King Lear*, Domenico in *Filumena* (Almeida Theatre); Stephano in *The Tempest*, Swanson in *Flare Path* (Theatre Royal Haymarket); title role in *Henry IV Parts 1 & 2*, Richard Plantagenet in *Henry VI Parts 1, 2 & 3*, Bolingbroke in *Richard II*, Sir Toby Belch in *Twelfth Night*, Macduff in *Macbeth*, Claudius in *Hamlet*, title role in *Pilate, Antony and Cleopatra, Much Ado About Nothing, Richard III*, Valmont in *Les Liaisons Dangereuses* (all Royal Shakespeare Company); Banquo in *Macbeth* (National Theatre).

Television includes *Casualty, Sense8, Father Brown, In The Dark, Wallander, Midsomer Murders, Utopia, Holby City, Endeavour, The Bible, Without You, Waking the Dead, Land Girls, The Pillars of the Earth, Eleventh Hour, A Touch of Frost, Dunkirk, The Lion in Winter, Death in Holy Orders, London's Burning, The Globe, Bonkers, Minder, Press Gang, Mr Palfry of Westminster, A Kind of Loving.*

Films include *Buster, Treasure Island, Red Mercury, The Innocent, Salmon Fishing in the Yemen, The Crucifer of Blood, Suffragette, All The Money In The World.*

Games: Pirate Lord in *Sea of Thieves*, Gothi in *Hellblade II*.

ANDREW WOODALL | Clement Attlee

Previously at Chichester: Duke of Norfolk in *The Other Boleyn Girl* (Festival Theatre), *First Light, South Downs/The Browning Version* (also West End), all Minerva Theatre.

Theatre credits include *Bloody Difficult Women* (Riverside Studios); *Great Britain* (also West End), *Women Beware Women, Much Ado About Nothing, The Life of Galileo, The Voysey Inheritance, Luther, Shape of the Table, Murmuring Judges, Racing Demon, Abingdon Square* (National Theatre); *Julius Caesar, Antony and Cleopatra, Wendy and Peter Pan* (RSC); *The Knowledge/Little Platoons* (Bush); *The Sugar Syndrome, Search and Destroy, Disappeared, Weldon Rising* (Royal Court); *Something in the Air, Admissions, As You Like It, As You Desire Me, A Letter of Resignation* (West End); *Gaslight, King Lear, Cloud Nine, Waste, The Provok'd Wife* (Old Vic); *Certain Young Men, Butterfly Kiss* (Almeida); *Hedda Gabler* (Gate, Dublin); *The Wars of the Roses* (Rose Theatre Kingston); *Don Carlos* (Glasgow Citizens); *Benefactors* (Sheffield Crucible); *The Art of Success* (Paines Plough).

Television includes *The Couple Next Door, The Reckoning, Lockwood & Co, Endeavour, Des, Lucan, Silk, Miranda, New Worlds, An Adventure in Space and Time, Hear the Silence, The Suspicions of Mr Whicher, New Tricks, Grantchester, Charles II, Kavanagh QC, Gimme Gimme Gimme, Dalziel & Pascoe, Heartbeat, Nature Boy, Seaforth, Degrees of Error, Prime Suspect III, Headhunters, Wish Me Luck, Hannay.*

Films include *Solo: A Star Wars Story, Where Is Anne Frank?, 303 Squadron, The Riot Club, Belle, Johnny English Reborn, Hypnotic, Count of Monte Cristo, Regeneration.*

CREATIVE

DEBORAH ANDREWS | Costume Designer and Costume Supervisor

Previously at Chichester as Costume Supervisor: *King Lear* and *The Winslow Boy*.

Costume Designs in theatre include *Henry IV* (Donmar Warehouse and St Ann's Warehouse NY) and *The Glass Piano* (The Coronet, London).

As Co-Costume Designer, work includes *Guys and Dolls* (The Bridge Theatre); *Patriots* (Almeida, West End and Broadway).

As Costume Associate Designer: *The Birthday Party* (West End); *The Doctor* (Almeida).

Work as Costume Supervisor in theatre includes *To Kill a Mockingbird, Prima Facie, Company, Spring Awakening, Ink, The Twilight Zone* (Almeida & West End); *London Tide, The Welkin, Angels in America* (also Broadway) (both National Theatre); in opera, *Katya Kabanova, Otello, Oklahoma* (Grange Park Opera); *Maria Luisa, Vanessa, The Rape of Lucretia, La bohème, St Matthew Passion* (Glyndebourne Festival Opera).

Studied Fashion Design at Central Saint Martin's College of Art.

CHRISTOPHE EYNDE | Associate Set Designer

Christophe is a set designer for theatre, opera, and dance productions. Other credits as an Associate Designer include *Your Lie in April* (Harold Pinter Theatre, London), *Detention* (Cast, Doncaster), and *Wild About You* (Theatre Royal Drury Lane, London). Internationally, Christophe was part of *Das Rheingold* (La Monnaie, Brussels) and is designing *Così Fan Tutte* for the Summer of Antwerp festival (Belgium).

Christophe holds an MSc in Architecture from KU Leuven and an MA in Scenography from the Royal Central School of Speech and Drama.

Instagram @christophe.eynde

JONATHAN KENT | Director

Previous productions at Chichester include *Sweet Bird of Youth*, David Hare's *Young Chekhov Trilogy* (and National Theatre), *Gypsy* (and West End), *Private Lives* (and West End), *Sweeney Todd* (and West End), *A Month in the Country*.

Between 1990 and 2002 Jonathan was joint Artistic Director of the Almeida Theatre, which he co-founded as a full-time producing theatre. His productions included *When We Dead Awaken*; *All for Love*; *Medea* (also West End/Broadway); *Chatsky*; *The Showman*; *The School for*

Wives; *Gangster No 1*; *Tartuffe*; *The Life of Galileo*; *The Rules of the Game*; *Ivanov* (also Moscow); *The Government Inspector*; *Naked* (also West End); *The Tempest*; *Hamlet* (also Broadway); *Richard II*; *Coriolanus* (also New York/Tokyo); *Phèdre*; *Britannicus* (also West End/New York); *Plenty* (West End); *Lulu* (also Washington); *Platonov* and *King Lear*.

Other theatre work includes *Double Feature* (Hampstead Theatre); *Aspects of Love* (Lyric Theatre, Shaftesbury Avenue); Florian Zeller's *The Forest* (Hampstead Theatre); *Talking Heads* (BBC TV, Bridge Theatre); *A German Life* (Bridge Theatre); *The Height of the Storm* (Wyndham's/Broadway); *Peter Gynt* (co-production with National Theatre and Edinburgh International Festival); *Slaves of Solitude* (Hampstead Theatre); *Good People* (Hampstead Theatre/West End); *Long Day's Journey into Night* (Broadway); *Le Cid, Mother Courage and Her Children, The False Servant, Oedipus* and *The Emperor and Galilean* (all National Theatre); *Man of La Mancha* (Broadway); *Hamlet* (Japan); *Hecuba* (Donmar); *Bond's Lear* (Sheffield Crucible); *As You Desire Me* (West End); *The Country Wife, The Sea* and *Marguerite* (all Theatre Royal Haymarket); *Faith Healer* (Dublin/Broadway).

Opera work includes *Elektra* and *Die Frau ohne Schatten* (both Mariinsky, St Petersburg); *The Fairy Queen* (Glyndebourne/Paris/New York); *Tosca* (Royal Opera House); *A Child of Our Time* and *The Flying Dutchman* (both ENO/Royal Danish Opera); *Lucio Silla*; *Kát'a Kabanová, The Tempest, The Marriage of Figaro* and *The Letter* (all Santa Fe); *The Turn of the Screw*; *Don Giovanni* and *Hippolyte et Aricie* (all Glyndebourne); and *Manon Lescaut* (Royal Opera House).

Jonathan has just completed a film of *Long Day's Journey into Night* with Jessica Lange and Ed Harris which is due for release this year.

HARRY MACKRILL | Dramaturg

Harry is a theatre director, dramaturg and researcher. He was Resident Director at the Tricycle Theatre (2013–2015), Associate Director at Kiln Theatre (2018–2019) and is co-founder and Creative Director of The Lot Productions.

As director: *What It Means* (The Lot/Wilton's); *Road* (Synergy Theatre Project); *World's End* (The Lot/King's Head); *Let Kilburn Shake* (Kiln Theatre); *Boy with Beer* (King's Head).

As dramaturg: *Burnt Sugar, The Housing Lark, What It Means* (The Lot); *The Orchard of Lost Souls* (Fio).

Harry is currently a Practice as Research PhD researcher at Leeds Beckett School of Arts, exploring the impact of Section 28 through actor training.

PETER MUMFORD | Lighting and Video Designer

Previous designs at Chichester include *Heartbreak House, The Last Confession, The Master and Margarita, A Midsummer Night's Dream, Out of This World* (Festival Theatre); *4000 Miles, 8 Hotels, The Stepmother, King Lear* (also BAM), *The Waltz of the Toreadors* (Minerva Theatre). Peter is a former CFT Lighting Design Associate.

Recent theatre designs include *Boys on the Verge of Tears* (Soho Theatre); *Rock 'n' Roll* (Hampstead); *Drop The Dead Donkey* (UK tour); *A Number* (Bridge Theatre); *Far Away* (Donmar); *Three Sisters* (National Theatre); *The Ferryman* (Royal Court/West End/Broadway); *42nd Street* (West End); *King Kong* (Global Creatures/Australia/Broadway); *My Name is Lucy Barton* (Bridge Theatre/Samuel J Friedman Theatre New York); *Ghosts* (Almeida/West End/BAM); *Long Day's Journey into Night* (West End/BAM).

Recent ballet designs: *Don Quixote* (Birmingham Royal Ballet); *Within the Golden Hour* (Rome/Monte-Carlo/Bordeaux); *Corybantic Games* (Royal Ballet).

Recent opera designs: *The Rake's Progress, L'incoronazione di Poppea* (Grange Festival); *Orfeo ed Euridice* (Staatsoper Hannover); *Pearl Fishers, Requiem* (Opera North); *Die Tote Stadt* (Opernhaus Düsseldorf); *Falstaff* (Greek National Opera); *Romeo et Juliette* (Teatro del Maggio Musicale Fiorentino); *Peter Grimes* (Paris/ROH/Madrid); *Madama Butterfly* (Vienna); *The Mask of Orpheus* (ENO).

Peter directed the concert staging and designed the lighting and projection for *Der Ring des Nibelungen* (which won the South Bank Sky Arts Opera Award) and *Der Fliegende Holländer* for Opera North; *Fidelio* (Garsington); *Die Walkure* (Lisbon); *Otello* (Bergen National Opera); and *Fidelio* (Orchestre de Chambre de Paris).

Awards include Olivier Award for Best Lighting Design (*The Bacchai*); Olivier Award for Outstanding Achievement in Dance; Knight of Illumination Award (*Sucker Punch*); Helpmann Award and Green Room Award for Best Lighting (*King Kong*). He was a double 2019 Tony nominee for Best Lighting Design for *The Ferryman* and *King Kong*.

www.petermumford.info

JOANNA PARKER | Set Designer

Also for Festival 2024: *The Other Boleyn Girl* (Festival Theatre).

Joanna Parker designs sets and costumes for theatre, opera and dance; her works have premiered in the UK, Europe and the USA.

Theatre: *Peculiar Journey through Time* (The Burg Theater , Vienna); *Translations, iGirl, Walls and Windows* (Abbey Theatre); *Much Ado About Nothing* (Shakespeare's Globe); *On Raftery's Hill* (Abbey Theatre);

The Noise of Time (Complicité/Lincoln Centre NY); *The Sarajevo Story* (Lyric Hammersmith); *American Buffalo* and *The Misanthrope* (Young Vic); *After Darwin* (Hampstead Theatre); *The Robbers* (Gate Theatre); *Off Camera* (West Yorkshire Playhouse); *Apache Tears* (Clean Break/ Battersea Arts).

Opera includes *The Requiem/After Tears* (and BBC film) and *The Pearl Fishers* (also Video Designs) and *Andrea Chenier* (Opera North); *Glass Human* (Glyndebourne on Tour); *Rodelinda, The Rape of Lucretia* (RCM); *Precipice, Carmen* (also Video Design & Movement, Grange Festival Opera); *Aida* (Opera North/Montpellier Opera); *Turandot* (Opera North/Teatro Nacional de São Carlos); *The Barber of Seville* (Glyndebourne Festival/tour/Malmo Opera); *The Commission, Café Kafka* (ROH & Aldeburgh Music); *The Two Widows* (Angers Nantes Opera); *Eugene Onegin, Flavio, A Midsummer Night's Dream, Alcina, The Marriage of Figaro* (English Touring Opera); *The Cunning Little Vixen* (Opera Theatre Company Dublin/Brno Festival Opera); *Friend of People* (Scottish Opera); *Giulio Cesare* (ROH).

joannaparker.org/selected-works

ANNELIE POWELL CDG | Casting Director
ALICE WALTERS | Casting Assistant

Also for Festival 2024: *Coram Boy* (Festival Theatre).

Theatre includes *Kathy and Stella Solve a Murder* (West End & UK tour); *Now That's What I Call a Musical* (ROYO/UK tour); *A Taste of Honey* (Royal Exchange); *Oliver!, In Dreams, Wendy and Peter Pan* (Leeds Playhouse); *Of Mice and Men, What's New Pussycat?* (Birmingham Rep); *Unexpected Twist, The Pope* (Royal & Derngate); *Alice's Adventures Underground* (Les Enfants Terribles); *The Other Place Fest* (RSC); *The Wonderful World of Dissocia* (Theatre Royal Stratford East); *One Man Two Guvnors* (NST/New Wolsey Theatre); *CinderELLA, The Shadow Factory* (NST); *The House of Shades, Vassa* (Almeida); *Faustus: That Damned Woman* (Headlong/Lyric Hammersmith); *The Weatherman* (Park Theatre); *Pavilion* (Theatr Clwyd); *Cougar* (Orange Tree/ETT); *Billionaire Boy, Fantastic Mr Fox* (NST & UK tours); *Othello* (UK tour & Dubai Opera); *Wolfie, Moone Disaster, Cotton Wool* (Theatre503); *The Audience* (Nuffield Theatre); *A Streetcar Named Desire* (NST/ Theatr Clwyd/ETT); *The Last Days of Anne Boleyn* (Tower of London); *Othello/Macbeth* (Lyric Hammersmith); *Don Carlos* (Rose Theatre/NST/ Northcott); *Babette's Feast* (Print Room); *Freedom on the Tyne* (Freedom City Newcastle); *Three Sisters* (Lyric Belfast); *The Summer Book, The Prince and the Pauper* (Unicorn Theatre); *I Killed Rasputin* (Assembly Rooms Edinburgh); *Even Stillness Breathes* (Soho); *Horrible Histories* (Birmingham Stage Company); *Dead Kid Songs* (Theatre Royal Bath); *but I cd only whisper, Boy on the Swing* (Arcola).

Television includes *Testament, The River Cruise Romances, Christmas in the Cotswolds, Rita* (UK Casting Director), *Goldie's Oldies, Trying* (Children's Casting Associate).

Films include *Dragonkeeper, Deep Blue Sea 3, Another Day of Life* and the shorts *I Remember You, Limbo, Thank You Hater!*

CHRISTOPHER SHUTT | Sound Designer

Previously at Chichester: *Murder on the Orient Express* (Festival Theatre), *The Inquiry, The Country Girls, The House of Special Purpose* (Minerva Theatre).

Theatre includes *Mnemonic, Drive your Plow Over the Bones of the Dead, A Disappearing Number, Elephant Vanishes, Noise of Time, Street of Crocodiles, Three Lives of Lucie Cabrol* (Complicite); *Macbeth* (found spaces); *Brokeback Mountain, Four Quartets, The Twilight Zone, Frozen, The Entertainer, The Winter's Tale, The Father* (West End); *War Horse, The Crucible, The Corn is Green, Paradise, Hansard, Top Girls, Antony and Cleopatra, Julie, John, Twelfth Night, Here We Go, Man and Superman, The James Plays (Parts I & II), From Morning to Midnight, Burnt By the Sun, Every Good Boy Deserves Favour, Coram Boy, Play Without Words, Machinal* (National Theatre); *The Treatment* (Almeida); *Glass. Kill. Bluebeard. Imp, ear for eye, Escaped Alone, Love and Information, Aunt Dan and Lemon, Serious Money, Road* (Royal Court); *Timon of Athens* (& New York/Washington), *Macbeth, Hamlet, Oppenheimer* (& West End), *The Two Gentlemen of Verona, Wendy and Peter Pan, The Tempest, King Lear* (all for RSC); *Far Away, St Nicholas, Aristocrats, Knives in Hens, Saint Joan, Faith Healer, Privacy, Philadelphia Here I Come!* (Donmar); *Timon of Athens, War Horse, A Human Being Died That Night, Macbeth, All My Sons, The Resistible Rise of Arturo Ui, Happy Days, A Moon for the Misbegotten, Coram Boy, Not About Nightingales, Mnemonic* (Broadway/NY); *Hamlet, Julius Caesar* (Barbican); *All About My Mother* (Old Vic).

Awards include Tony Award (*War Horse*), Evening Standard Theatre Award (*A Disappearing Number*), New York Drama Desk Award (*War Horse, Mnemonic, Not About Nightingales*).

SYDNEY STEVENSON | Assistant Director

Directing includes *Britain's Happiest Woman* (short film), *The Three Musketeers* (workshop).

As Assistant Director: *Betrayal* (Theatre Royal Bath), *The Three Musketeers – Attempted by Foolhardy* (also writer, online), *1984* (ArtsEd), *Set Me Free* and *Halcyon Heights* (short films).

Writing includes *Thicker Than Water* (winner of the UKTV and Female Pilot club female writers initiative), *Old Bag* (short film), *Fool* (series currently in development), *Next Door – An Awkward Love Story* (Tabard Theatre), *M*n and Women* (winner of the Voices from Home Competition with Broken Silence Theatre, The Old Red Lion), *Bubonic* (longlisted for the Papatango Prize and workshopped with ATG).

As an actor, theatre includes *Relatively Speaking* (The Mill at Sonning), *Next Door* (Tabard Theatre), *The Men from the Ministry* (White Bear Theatre), *Beauty and the Beast* and *Aladdin* (Hawthorne Theatre), *The Three Musketeers* (The Other Palace). On TV: *Doctors, Misfits, Red Dwarf, Me and Mrs Jones, My Family*; on Film: *Old Bag, Love & Spirit, Resting*.

PAUL UNWIN | Writer

Plays include *Theory For The Attention Of Mr Einstein* (Old Red Lion, Frankfurt Stadt theatre), *Doolaly Days* (Leicester, tour, Hampstead New End), *This Much Is True – The Killing of Jean Charles de Menezes* (Theatre 503), *At The Point Of Need* (Old Vic) and *The Enfield Haunting* (Ambassadors Theatre).

As Artistic Director of the Bristol Old Vic, productions include *In The Ruins* (Bristol Old Vic/Royal Court); *The Misanthrope* (Bristol Old Vic/National Theatre); *Hamlet, Othello, Uncle Vanya, The Clandestine Marriage, The Life of Galileo, The Three Sisters, The Cherry Orchard, Tartuffe, In Times Like These* (by Jeremy Brock) and *The Three Musketeers. A Town in the West Country* involved three hundred Bristolians and was the subject of an ITV South Bank Show. Worked closely with Arthur Miller on the European premieres of *The Man Who Had All The Luck* (Bristol Old Vic and Young Vic) and *The Archbishop's Ceiling*.

Freelance productions include *Uncle Vanya* (Gate Theatre Dublin), *Loot* (Royal Exchange, Manchester) and *The Misanthrope* (Cambridge Theatre).

His short film *Syrup* was nominated for an Oscar and a BAFTA, won the Cannes Jury Prize and Amnesty International Award. He directed *The American* with Matthew Modine and Diana Rigg for BBC films. His film *Elijah* won the Gemini and Leo Awards in Canada.

As a TV director, productions include *The Bill, EastEnders*, Rik Mayall in *Claire de Lune* and *Dirty Old Town, The Bare Necessities, Bramwell, Combat Hospital, NCS, Poirot, Miss Marple, Messiah* and *Casualty.*

Breathless co-created with Peter Grimsdale, directed opening and wrote the bulk of the series.

Casualty and *Holby City* co-created with Jeremy Brock. *Casualty* has won six RTS awards and seven BAFTAS.

Currently, working on *58 Seconds* with Jeremy Brock and *Heroes/Berlin* for German TV.

GARY YERSHON | Composer

Gary Yershon's stage scores include many productions for the Royal Shakespeare Company, National Theatre, West End and Broadway; including the English-language premieres of Yasmina Reza's *Art*, *The Unexpected Man*, *Life x 3* and *God of Carnage*; *Julius Caesar* (Donmar Warehouse); Florian Zeller's *The Height of the Storm* (Wyndham's); and *The Norman Conquests* (Old Vic/New York: Drama Desk award nomination). Previously at Chichester, *The Water Babies*, *Wild Orchids*, *The Recruiting Officer* and *The Magistrate* (all Festival Theatre).

Dance includes *Ma Vie en Rose* (Young Vic), *The Boy in the Striped Pyjamas* (Northern Ballet).

Television includes *Trial and Retribution IX & X*, *James the Cat*, *Ebb and Flo*.

Radio includes *The Odyssey*, *Gawain and the Green Knight*, *The Theban Plays*, *The Winter's Tale*, *Autumn Journal*.

Films include Mike Leigh's *Topsy-Turvy* (as musical director), *Happy-Go Lucky*, *Another Year* (European Film Award nomination), *A Running Jump*, *Mr Turner* (Moët et Chandon/Camille Award for Best Orchestral Score, and nominations for an Ivor Novello Award, ASCAP Composer's Choice award, and Academy Award for Best Original Score), *Peterloo* and *Hard Truths*.

Concert works include *The Great Blueness*, commissioned and premiered by the London Symphony Orchestra; *Lockdown Variations* for solo flute; the wind quintet *Ready for Anything*; the septet *Metamorphonie* for the City of Nîmes; and *Islands*, a suite for French horn, violin and piano, for the Trio Arisonto.

Having begun his career as an actor-musician, Gary returned to live performance in 2019 with a series of shows at Crazy Coqs.

Gary is an Associate Artist of the RSC and the Old Vic, an Associate Teacher at RADA, and a guest lecturer at the London Film School. He is a member of the Academy of Motion Picture Arts and Sciences and the European Film Academy.

garyyershon.com

CHARACTERS

Based on real people:

ELLEN WILKINSON – In her mid-fifties, she is a powerful, passionate woman. The only woman in the 1945 Labour Cabinet.

CLEMENT ATTLEE – In his early sixties. Stiff, diffident but a cool political operator.

VIOLET ATTLEE – Attlee's wife. Upper-middle-class and dynamic.

HERBERT MORRISON – In his late fifties. A politician to his marrow.

ERNIE BEVIN – Mid-sixties. A powerful old school Labour and Union politician. Loyal.

NYE BEVAN – Mid-fifties. A charismatic and inspiring insurgent.

JENNIE LEE – Early fifties. More than Bevan's wife – one of the great Labour MPs. Scottish, vivacious.

HUGH DALTON – Late fifties. Four square, tough, arrogant.

RICHARD STAFFORD CRIPPS – Late fifties, possibly feels older. Has an edgy fragility, but a formidable intellect.

LORD MORAN (CHARLIE WILSON) – A senior doctor.

WINSTON CHURCHILL

Invented:

JOAN VINCENT – A young black Labour Party worker.

THOMAS MERRIMAN – A young architecture student.

YOUNG PHOTOGRAPHER

LABOUR PARTY WORKERS

A SENIOR NURSE

A DOCTOR

WAITERS

A BOY SINGER

AUTHOR'S NOTE

The Promise is set in England between the 25th of May 1945 and 7th of February 1947.

Although *The Promise* is based on detailed research and all but two of the characters are inspired by real people, the play is a work of imagination.

For Katie, with all my love.

ACT ONE

Scene One

(Dolphin Square, London/the Blackpool Winter Gardens.)

(The setting is spare but beautiful. A wall and a floor are made of wood. They have lustre and depth. A **WOMAN** *with red hair lies foetal centre stage. She is dressed in a delicate silk kimono. Snow swirls around her. Shouts offstage.)*

PORTER 1. You tried knocking?

PORTER 2. She's not answering…

(The sound of knocking. A third voice – young working-class Londoner – **JOAN VINCENT***.)*

JOAN. Miss? Miss?

*(***ELLEN WILKINSON*** *stands behind a collection of microphones. She is small but powerful and driven.)*

ELLEN. Conference, our people have been through dark times. We have been through dark times. Our people have been challenged to their core. They have felt dread. They have experienced terrible loss. But listen. Do you hear that? No air raid sirens. Just a fun fair on the promenade! A child laughing! This has been a war that has hit at the heart of our country and of our people.

ELLEN. We are gathered here in Blackpool to remember, to pay gratitude, but most, to look forward.

(The knocking grows.)

JOAN. Miss? Miss? Can you hear us?

ELLEN. Today, conference, we face a choice. Through the war, Labour put to one side our vision of the kind of society we dream of and got on with the urgent business of saving our entire way of life from evil. We have been in a coalition government with Mr Churchill and have served shoulder to shoulder with men who otherwise would be our bitter enemies. But now, conference, the question we face is: do we go on playing second fiddle? Or do we fight for a Labour future...?

(Knocking. **JOAN**'s *voice is now desperate.)*

JOAN. Open the door, please, please!

ELLEN. We know an election will be a vicious fight. But can we ignore what we have learned? Remember how the Conservatives promised half a million new homes after the Great War? They didn't build seven hundred! They promised jobs! A year after the Armistice? Over two million men were unemployed, and hundreds of thousands of our people were short of food.

(She's now flying.)

Can we go through that again? No! No! No! There will be those here who will say now is not the time. The Tories will call us Communists. Revolutionaries! Their newspapers will attack us. But I say conference: VOTE. Vote for today's motion to smash our coalition with Conservative Mr Churchill, end the National Government and turn to face the country in a General Election as a Labour Party. We have a chance to take power. That chance may not come again in our lifetime.

Win this election, and we have a real hope of building in Britain, on these beloved islands, the civilisation we so passionately desire, and our people so deserve.

> *(Applause and the thumping on the door continue until...)*

Scene Two

(The Admiral's Bar at the Blackpool Grand.)

(Labour Party Conference, May 1945. Dance music off. **CLEMENT ATTLEE** *sits in front of a* **YOUNG PHOTOGRAPHER**. **CLEM** *is stiff and diffident. His wife* **VIOLET** *is upper-middle-class and dynamic. The* **PHOTOGRAPHER***'s camera flashes.)*

VIOLET. Oh, Clem, not the pipe.

CLEM. No one will recognise me without my pipe.

VIOLET. Chin up, then.

(Private.) You look exhausted.

> *(He is.)*

Well at least do sit up straight.

> *(The* **PHOTOGRAPHER** *adjusts something. He is nervous facing such a famous man.)*

CLEM. You from round here, lad?

PHOTOGRAPHER. *(Lancastrian.)* Sir.

CLEM. I imagine you would rather be photographing donkey rides on the beach.

PHOTOGRAPHER. Oh no, Mr Attlee.

VIOLET. Well, do say cheese, Clem.

> *(Flash!* **ERNIE BEVIN** *arrives carrying chips. He's a powerful man dressed in an enormous overcoat.)*

---

* A licence to produce *THE PROMISE* does not include a performance license for any third-party or copyrighted recordings. Licensees should create their own.

ERNIE. The Labour Party is a pitiful collection of holier-than-thou, bloody fools. No, they are worse than that. We are going to need to keep our strength up: chip, Clem? Violet?

VIOLET. Oh. No, no. Thank you, though, Mr Bevin.

ERNIE. Lad?

(*The* **PHOTOGRAPHER** *is awestruck by* **ERNIE.***)*

Either shut your mouth or put a chip in it.

(*The* **PHOTOGRAPHER** *takes a chip.*)

Do you like fireworks? There's going to be a display on the Pier any second now. You don't want to miss them, do you, lad?

(*Getting the prompt, the* **PHOTOGRAPHER** *picks up his things.*)

PHOTOGRAPHER. Yes, sir.

CLEM. *(To the* **PHOTOGRAPHER.***)* Best of everything.

PHOTOGRAPHER. And good luck, Mr Attlee.

(*He goes.*)

CLEM. Super chap.

ERNIE. *(Coming in hard.)* This is insanity, Clem. We cannot let them dissolve the National Government.

CLEM. But conference voted…

ERNIE. (Loud.) The fighting in Germany is only just finished. It is all over-excited nonsense, you know that.

VIOLET. Please, Ernie, the poor man is exhausted. You are Clem!

ERNIE. I'm sorry but if we go to the country now we will lose. You…we…need to put a stop to this before…

(He stops as **ELLEN** *and* **HERBERT MORRISON** *appear. She has a pronounced limp. They are both breathing hard from dancing.)*

HERBERT. *(Suave.)* Violet, why have you hidden Clem away in here!?

*(***VIOLET*** is about to speak when...)*

ELLEN. Wow, Mr Morrison. That was quite a spin he took me on.

ERNIE. Dancing is suicidal at our age.

HERBERT. What a perfect conference! It was a real rally. It pulled the party together.

CLEM. Our chairwoman was most rousing!

ERNIE. Miss Wilkinson, has roused a party of lemmings.

ELLEN. Oh, Ernie, smile. Try it every once in a while.

(But she starts to gasp for air.)

ERNIE. Why would I smile? You have cajoled us into taking on Britain's most beloved leader, since Queen Elizabeth saw off the Armada. Insanity...

*(***ELLEN*** can't breathe.)*

Ellen?

ELLEN. M-y ch-est is m-y Achilles.

*(***ELLEN*** tries to look like this is nothing serious, but she is gasping...)*

VIOLET. Let me get you some water.

ELLEN. It's n-o-thing!

HERBERT. Miss Wilkinson, a chair, let me...

ELLEN. I'm f-f-ine – for p-p-ity's sake!

*(**ELLEN** is now breathing easier.)*

ERNIE. I blame you, Herbert – jitterbuggering away like that...

ELLEN. I led Mr Morrison, Ernie! Herbert dances like my father did. Summat from the bar and I'll be 100 percent.

*(Grinning, **ELLEN** lights a cigarette.)*

CLEM. Ellen, what can I set you up with?

*(He stands – but is stopped by **ERNIE** going.)*

ERNIE. The war with the Japanese is not over! What's the damn rush?

ELLEN. None of us are going to live forever, and this is our best chance...

ERNIE. We cannot defeat Winston. Certainly not with nearly half million lads still fighting in the Pacific. It is insanity. Insanity. I am sorry Ellen, but it bloody well is.

MORRISON. *(Calm.)* With proper organisation and leadership throughout the party I – and I know many Comrades – agree with Miss Wilkinson: this is our moment. Ernie, we can organise the service vote! Easily. Clem could we drag you away just for a moment...

VIOLET. *(Changing the subject.)* Do you know, Mr Attlee and my ancient bones are so enjoying a constitution every morning. The sea air, the promenade. And to watch the young, at last, relaxing! Really marvellous.

ELLEN. *(Keeping it light.)* I'm never convinced by seagulls, Mrs Attlee.

(Turning.) Clem if you wouldn't mind...

VIOLET. But why did you both have to go all the way to San Francisco! I simply cannot understand why the United Nations couldn't have met in Bognor Regis, for, example. Perfectly nice hotels. Clean carpets.

ERNIE. *(Laughing.)* If the rooms in Blackpool guest houses and hotels could talk!

HERBERT. And what exactly is that supposed to mean?

ERNIE. Touched a nerve, Morrison?

> *(There is absolutely no love lost between* **ERNIE** *and* **HERBERT**.*)*

HERBERT. Clem – if we could just discuss this, Ellen and I...

ERNIE. Give me strength.

> *(He takes out a hip flask and drinks.)*

ELLEN. San Francisco was wonderful wasn't it Clem? The talk. And the people.

CLEM. *(Enthused.)* It was quite something! The world is changing. Really!

VIOLET. *(Interrupting.)* AAnd then the moment you both staggered off those frightful aeroplanes, Mr Attlee was off again – you were, my dear. It's no good looking at your shoes like that –

> *(***CLEM*** <u>is</u> looking at his shoes.)*

to Berlin with Winston. And the girls are home pining for their father. Clem is exhausted. Enough.

CLEM. *(Smiling.)* A couple of hours deadheading will put everything to rights.

ELLEN. *(Firm.)* Clem, Herbert and I really would like a...

CLEM. Your drink! Oh gosh, Ellen, how terribly rude of me.

> *(***CLEM*** turns to go to the bar. **HERBERT** and* **ELLEN** *start to follow, but* **ERNIE** *is suddenly blocking her way.* **VIOLET** *moves to* **ELLEN**'s *other flank.)*

ERNIE. Lass.

VIOLET. A little birdy tells me you've moved into a flat in Dolphin Square. Is it really full of spies and mistresses? How thrilling.

ELLEN. Maiden aunts and rather handsome officers from the Household Cavalry, more like. Will you excuse me – I'd like to join Mr Attlee and Herbert…

ERNIE. *(About* **HERBERT** *and* **CLEM.***)* Skulduggery, Miss Wilkinson??

ELLEN. Just dull procedural business! Herbert wants Clem…

VIOLET. *(Lethal.)* Youngest of ten, I developed a nose for liars before I could speak Ellen.

> *(A firework goes off outside.)*

ERNIE. *(Calling.)* We should show our faces, Clem!

ELLEN. I'll wait for Mr Morrison.

ERNIE. Everyone will think it's the Blitz having a final parade. Ellen, your appearance will calm the foot soldiers. Come.

VIOLET. I loathe fireworks: vile noise, squeals of delight. All rather pointless. Come on.

> *(Reluctantly,* **ELLEN** *follows* **VIOLET** *and* **ERNIE***. Fireworks.)*

HERBERT. Clem, you know where I stand in the Party, don't you?

CLEM. The centre. And, I must tell you, Winston thinks you have been an outstanding Home Secretary.

HERBERT. London is mine…

CLEM. And, as you say, London is yours.

HERBERT. Churchill will make mincemeat of us and ride straight back into Number 10…

> *(***CLEM** *has the drinks.)*

CLEM. Oh. They've gone.

(Earnest, to **HERBERT**.*)* I'm not sure I don't agree with Ernie that breaking with the National government is folly. Will the people forgive us? Your political instincts are terribly sharp.

HERBERT. *(This is the moment.)* Clem, you won't win, not against Winston. You can't win.

CLEM. But Conference has voted...

HERBERT. Yes! For us to break with Winston. But to win, we need change. I want the leadership.

CLEM. Oh, I know what you want, Herbert, but there isn't a vacancy, don't you see?

(Fireworks outside.)

Scene Three

(A Blackpool hotel room.)

(The thump-thump-thump and fireworks evolve – the sounds could now be footsteps. Indistinguishable voices off – the mental chatter of insomnia, a bed, and a bedside light. **ELLEN** *is in bed.)*

ELLEN. *(Loud.)* Will you go ta'yer bed? Can we get some rest? Can we get some sleep?

(Desperate, she pulls the pillow over her head. There is a tap on the door.)

For pity's sake, it's nearly five AM!

*(***ELLEN** *reaches for her kimono. There is more noise around the room. The tap, again.* **ELLEN** *opens the door.* **HERBERT** *is holding his shoes. He smiles.)*

Not sure what you're grinning about Herbert.

(Noise from the next room.)

HERBERT. Gawd – he's up early... Ellen, I can't stay in the corridor! Really, someone might see...

ELLEN. Then go back to your room.

HERBERT. Ellen, don't be angry. Not tonight. It was the wrong moment, that's all.

*(***HERBERT** *slips into the room.)*

I feel so alive.

ELLEN. And I just want some sleep.

(More noise from next room.)

ELLEN. He's been pacing all night. My head feels like it's going to explode. You should go.

(**HERBERT** *feels the silk of* **ELLEN**'s *kimono.*)

HERBERT. This is nice.

ELLEN. You ought to be with your wife, Herbert.

HERBERT. She caught the train to London the moment Attlee finished his speech. Duty done.

(*He tries to kiss her.*)

ELLEN. Damn near cleaned me out of dollars. In my next life I'm going to make a fortune importing lingerie for the socialist woman. You are married.

HERBERT. It is the coldest place you can imagine. Her contempt for me.

ELLEN. Margaret doesn't have contempt for you.

HERBERT. You've never been in a marriage that is dying, Ellen.

ELLEN. I've never been in a marriage at all, which may be the secret.

(**HERBERT** *presses against* **ELLEN**.)

If you are going to lead the party, we have to be careful. Very.

HERBERT. The war is bloody nearly over. Everything is different! Ellen, come on...

ELLEN. Listen to me: you do have a lot of support right through the Party...

HERBERT. Clem said I had great political instincts.

ELLEN. I wouldn't bet more than five bob, but we might just win this election.

HERBERT. With the right leader, a slender majority is possible, I suppose, Ellen. At a push.

ELLEN. With Clem gone, you could be Prime Minister, I suppose, Mr Morrison. At a push.

HERBERT. *(Not seeing she's playing him.)* I know. You are right. It is my time. But what about you? What will you want, Ellen?

ELLEN. What I've always wanted: a socialist government that creates a radically different country.

HERBERT. I rather meant what ministry? In Whitehall? With a driver...

> (**HERBERT** *presses against her.*)

ELLEN. Bloody heck, Herbert, no. Get some sleep.

HERBERT. I'm not at all tired.

> *(There's more noise – thump-thump-thump – from next door.)*

ELLEN. *(Laughing.)* It's Winston – the crafty old bugger – come to spy on Conference. Can you smell that? His cigar smoke?

> (**HERBERT** *sniffs.*)

I'm joking – it's some insomniac door-to-door salesman. Been up all night. I've not slept.

HERBERT. Everyone is so drunk downstairs the King and Queen could walk through the bar and no one would notice us. It's nearly dawn. Come on, Ellen, just once: together. Let's watch the sun come up. Let's stand on the beach – hand in hand – and breathe in tomorrow.

ELLEN. *(Laughing.)* Are you getting romantic in yer old age? What a terrifying bloody thought.

Scene Four

(The basement of the TGWU building.)

*(Typewriters. **JOAN**, 20, a working-class Londoner. A young student – **THOMAS MERRIMAN**, 22 – types painfully slowly with two fingers while a female **LABOUR PARTY WORKER** is rattling away.)*

JOAN. I thought you said you could type.

*(**THOMAS** stubbornly continues. She reads over his shoulder.)*

And spell. Is that how you spell 'technical'? Let me.

*(She pulls the paper out of the typewriter. **THOMAS** stands. **HERBERT** – in waistcoat and shirtsleeves – announces:)*

HERBERT. Half an hour, comrades, before this has to be type-set. Industry, who's got industry?

*(**THOMAS** goes to the table – and starts urgently searching.)*

JOAN. Mr Morrison, give us five secs, sir.

*(She is retyping **THOMAS**'s work.)*

HERBERT. *(Loud.)* INDUSTRY! If you don't mind, who?

JOAN. It's not quite...

HERBERT. Probably best to have it before Christmas.

*(**ELLEN** is magnificent in a fur coat. Smoking, watching.)*

ELLEN. *(Calm down.)* Mr Morrison.

JOAN. Right, sir, here we are!

> *(Reading.)*

"The Labour Party submits to the nation the following industrial programme..."

HERBERT. *(Impatient.)* No, girl, no. Just get to the end, please.

JOAN. "...the coal industry, producing Britain's most precious raw material, has been floundering chaotically and when the great economic blizzards swept the..."

HERBERT. "Great economic blizzards"? That just sounds miserable. And cold.

ELLEN. Before the war *was* miserable and cold.

HERBERT. Going on about 'The Great Depression' isn't going to get us votes.

ELLEN. People know the truth. They lived through it.

HERBERT. *(To* **JOAN**.*)* On. Type it. It will do. Come on, will you all!

> *(He looks at his watch.* **JOAN**, **THOMAS** *and the others sort and type.)*

ELLEN. No, no, Mr Morrison, what d'you want to say? Let's get it right.

HERBERT. The manifesto has to be reasonable. Realistic. And positive.

ELLEN. It is reasonable. And realistic and positive.

HERBERT. Men read these things carefully.

ELLEN. So we *don't* tell them we are going to tear down the slums?

HERBERT. Not till we know we have the money to rebuild new housing stock, no.

ELLEN. We have to capture people's imaginations.

HERBERT. People in Guildford don't have imaginations.

>   (**ELLEN** *notices* **JENNIE LEE**. *Scottish, ten years younger, vivacious.*)

ELLEN. Jennie! I thought you were in Cannock.

JENNIE. I missed London's grime and the political cut'n'thrust.

>   *(To* **ELLEN**, *as they embrace.)* A comradely debate, I see.

ELLEN. A man-hating being told 'owt. You well? You look well.

JENNIE. *(Taking off her coat.)* It's like an oven in here…

ELLEN. Well, I'm freezing. I keep badgering the jobsworth in charge of resources to turn the heat up. "Every temperature alteration must be in triplicate."

>   *(She pops pills into her mouth.)*

JENNIE. Ellen?

ELLEN. *(Ignoring* **JENNIE***'s concern.)* Mr Morrison, what should Miss Lee take?

JENNIE. *(Surprised to be asked.)* Oh, I was just passing…

ELLEN. All hands to the pumps. According to Mr Morrison, we are taking on water, drowning in gloom!

JENNIE. I'd really like to see what I can do with health, Mr Morrison, if that's helpful.

HERBERT. *(Polite under pressure.)* Health? Actually, Ellen's nailed down the health section, haven't you, Miss Wilkinson?

>   (**ELLEN** *crosses to* **HERBERT**.)

ELLEN. Jennie is standing again as an MP. I'm sure she can massage a paragraph or two.

HERBERT. Oh fuck no. Please no. NO.

> (**HERBERT** *has realised* **NYE BEVAN** *has appeared.* **NYE** *smiles at* **JOAN**, *who is typing. He is charming. He wears a rough 'workingman's suit'.*)

NYE. I never mastered those infernal machines.

JOAN. Sir?

HERBERT. *(Whispering about* **NYE**.*)* Ellen, I really think we should not...

> (*But* **ELLEN** *ignores him, correcting a page.*)

NYE. Rank? Serial number? Typist first class, that is clear.

JOAN. I don't have a... Oh, you're joking around. Sorry, Mr Bevan.

> (**THOMAS** *leaps up – and puts his hand out to* **NYE** *and then salutes.*)

THOMAS. Thomas Merriman, sir. A real privilege and an honour...

> (**NYE** *looks at him – startled by* **THOMAS**'*s enthusiasm.*)

I fear I exaggerated my typing skills to get here.

> (**THOMAS** *goes back to sorting papers.* **NYE** *now smiles at* **HERBERT**.*)*

NYE. W-ell I'm clearly as w-welcome as a fox in a c-chicken c-coop!

> (**NYE** *has a stutter. He deals with it by over-enunciating.* **ELLEN** *turns, 'surprised' he is there.*)

ELLEN. Ah, don't be an idiot, Nye! You are welcome! This is our own personal bunker! Safe from strafing Tories.

*(**HERBERT** can hardly believe **ELLEN**'s welcome
but – a politician to his marrow – switches:)*

HERBERT. Good to see you. Nye. Great. We are almost ready.

(To the room.) Type-setting in under fifteen minutes,
everyone!

NYE. Don't mind me. I heard rumour of a tea trolley. With
biscuits.

ELLEN. *(To **NYE**.)* How's Ebbw Vale?

JENNIE. Even the sheep vote for him.

ELLEN. *(To **NYE**.)* We need you down here.

HERBERT. Well, Miss Wilkinson, we *are* nearly finished,
matter of fact. Just need to collate...

ELLEN. Nye, you've been on the outside for too long.

HERBERT. *(Easy, but alert.)* Mr Bevan has had a perfectly
good war agitating from the back benches, isn't that
right?

NYE. I have led the Parliamentary Labour Party while you
fraternised with your friend Churchill.

HERBERT. *(Oh, not this again.)* He's not my friend.

NYE. You could have fooled me!

JENNIE. Nye, is this really the moment?

ELLEN. *(Interrupting, firm.)* Churchill is a man we admire.
We should *all* admire.

NYE. Is that why you supported him crushing trade unions?

JENNIE. And they are off! Tin helmets on.

HERBERT. *(Loud, clear.)* No. No. Stop this. We don't need
this. Not *now*. Stop.

*(Pause, **NYE** can't resist...)*

NYE. But, as you well know, YOUR National Government put untrained boys in the mines instead of working men. And you banned strikes.

HERBERT. "Sorry, Mr Hitler, but we aren't coming out to fight until we can get better pay and bacon butties for our tea!" For pity's sake, Bevan...

ELLEN. *(Placating.)* Nye, you challenging the conduct of the war in the House was right, but now...

NYE. *(To* **HERBERT.***)* You were the Home Secretary in a *Tory* Government! That makes you responsible...

HERBERT. A *National* Government – to win the fucking war!

JENNIE. Nye stop. You are simply picking a fight.

ERNIE. Miss Lee is right.

> *(No one had noticed* **ERNIE** *in his coat in the shadows.)*

You are picking a fight, Bevan.

> *(Everyone goes back to work.)*

HERBERT. Ten minutes...

> *(He turns to* **THOMAS.***)*

Have you counted the sections, Mr Meredith?

THOMAS. Merriman, sir...

> *(***THOMAS** *hasn't – he panics and starts, counting under his breath.* **NYE** *has picked up a page and read it.)*

NYE. Dear God, but this isn't good enough, you know.

> *(Everyone looks up. He grabs the pencil from* **JENNIE***'s hand.)*

JENNIE. Nye, what do you think you are doing?

NYE. *(Ignoring her.)* You can't just say we *hope* to have good food, good homes and a free pint for every soldier returning.

(Reading.) "...the best health service..."

   (He scratches it out.)

HERBERT. Ah, well, the lucky old Tories will at least have a manifesto!

NYE. But this is waffle, Mr Morrison. Blah-de-blah. Piffle. MEANINGLESS. Don't you think?

JENNIE. Nye, you could easily have left it at waffle...

ELLEN. What *should* we say?

HERBERT. *(Loud.)* Ellen, no. That man is an agitator...

ELLEN. But "men read these things very carefully", isn't that so? Maybe we should get it right?

NYE. *(About the pages.)* None of this is new. You need specifics. Read this, and it's almost apologetic. There is nothing to be apologetic about.

ERNIE. To win this election, I'd say, our people need to know we are not living in cloud cuckoo land.

NYE. Is it cuckoo land to make people a promise, Mr Bevin?

ELLEN. No – but it needs to be something that we can defend. Under pressure, Nye.

NYE. Not *HOW* we are going to make their lives better? Surely even you can defend welfare, working conditions, opportunity for education, decent health care, no?

HERBERT. Oh so the tedious niceties of getting elected shouldn't trouble us...

NYE. Niceties! End rationing? Housing? Warm schools, children whose teeth don't chatter from hunger? Prove to the working people the country will be theirs, and they will vote for you.

*(**HERBERT** stares at **NYE**. Throughout, **THOMAS** has been counting sections. **HERBERT** smiles.)*

HERBERT. You are right, Nye, as always. OK? Happy? Because right now, I just want to get this to the printers.

NYE. The people have got used to being lied to by the Government. They have become passive, confused, exhausted. They are numb having being told lies, half-truths, and fed propaganda.

JENNIE. Nye what has this got to do with anything? Come on...

NYE. *(Louder.)* And I reckon something else: the people *know* what they were told was not true, but it's easier to doff their caps and go along with whatever that old windbag with his cigar and fancy dress said.

ELLEN. It was a war – so we worked with the Tories and Mr Churchill. A National Government. Yes, we had to...

NYE. Well, so long as you didn't get lost, Ellen. You were someone – you were a true socialist beacon. Before. But in the war?

(Hard.) Forgive me, but you forgot yourself. Really.

*(**ELLEN** stares at him. **JENNIE** breaks the silence.)*

JENNIE. His mother loves him, or so she says. Nye, they have re-hung the Cannelettos at the National Gallery. Come along, before the tea time crowds. I'm sorry, Ellen...

NYE. *(Not budging.)* You have nothing to apologise for.

JENNIE. *(Snapping, to **NYE**.)* But I think maybe *you* do.

NYE. No, Ellen, you see, I don't think we should change. Principles. They are everything. Or maybe I am just too much of an old school, honest to God, socialist for you and Mr Morrison's modern Labour Party?

ERNIE. I recognise you, Sonny.

JENNIE. Try having him be the first thing you see when you open your eyes. Enough, Nye...

NYE. Publish that so-called manifesto, and we'll be back on the opposition benches listening to the bloody Tories for the rest of our pitiful lives. Good afternoon.

> (**NYE** *and* **JENNIE** *leave.*)

HERBERT. He is insufferable.

ERNIE. The coming man often is.

> (**ELLEN** *is with* **JOAN**, **HERBERT** *paces.*
> **THOMAS** *counts sections.*)

ELLEN. *(To* **JOAN**, *about a page.)* I think maybe change that. Yes, take out the opening sentence.

HERBERT. Ellen, you know we can't have people like that near the centre.

ELLEN. *(Ignoring him.)* What brings you down here, Miss...?

JOAN. Vincent. Joan. Miss Wilkinson.

ELLEN. *(Warm.)* So why are you here, Joan?

JOAN. Oh, you know.

ELLEN. I'm not sure I do.

> (**JOAN** *looks at her – she has a lot locked
> away and is in awe of* **ELLEN**.)

JOAN. No. Well, I'd never fit in serving tea in a Lyons Corner House, so I did secretarial school but didn't fancy working for a sweaty businessman.

> (*She looks at* **ELLEN**.)

Anyway, after being told 'no' so many times, even I got the message.

ELLEN. Well, we are very lucky to have you, Joan.

JOAN. And, anyway, this really matters, doesn't it? And working for you, Miss Wilkinson, of course.

THOMAS. Sir. That's sixteen sections we are just waiting on...

HERBERT. *(Loud, he wants to sort this.)* Miss Wilkinson!

> **(HERBERT** *smiles; he's gone too far. He turns to* **THOMAS.***)*

Put them in the box, lad, over there.

(To **ELLEN.***)* Ellen, even Jennie Lee can't tame Bevan. Do you hear me, Ellen?

JOAN. Shall I hunt down the tea, Miss Wilkinson?

ELLEN. *(To* **JOAN.***)* I'll sort. Thanks though.

(To **HERBERT**, *furious.)* And perhaps you want to check your temper, Mr Morrison; I am not sure it becomes you.

> *(She goes.)*

ERNIE. You know what I learned on the docks, Herbert? Only pick fights you are certain you can win.

Scene Five

(Attlee's garden – Stanmore.)

(Bird song. Cane chairs near a table. The table has papers on it. In the house, a phone starts to ring. **VIOLET** *appears, hurrying.)*

VIOLET. *(Calling.)* Clem! Clem!

*(***ERNIE*** *appears. He's mopping his brow.)*

ERNIE. *(Urgent.)* Where is he?

CLEM. *(Offstage.)* Howzat!

ERNIE. What on earth?

VIOLET. Oh, for pity's sake.

(Calling.) Clem, Clem will you come here now!

ERNIE. The cars are here.

VIOLET. He's nervous. He always plays cricket with the children when he's nervous.

*(***CLEM*** *appears. He is sweaty, in shirt, tie, trousers – cricket ball.)*

CLEM. Alison is developing into a really rather tidy young bowler. I have been showing her the gully spin and the infamous Attlee googly. Marvellous.

(The phone starts to ring again in the house.)

VIOLET. You must get dressed.

ERNIE. The cars are here. I wish someone would pick up that telephone.

*(***CLEM*** *doesn't move.)*

VIOLET. Clem?

ERNIE. We should crack on.

VIOLET. I suppose one should think this is good news.

(*A doorbell rings.* **CLEM** *stuffs his pipe.*)

ERNIE. Clem? Violet? Come on.

CLEM. Surely, even I am allowed one last smoke.

VIOLET. No. Get dressed.

ERNIE. Cummon. I want to get you to the count. And then to the King.

CLEM. But what about Winston?

ERNIE. He'll no longer be Prime Minister, Clem.

CLEM. We owe everything to Winston Churchill. We must not forget that, Ernie. And the people love him.

ERNIE. Not enough, it seems.

(*The doorbell again.*)

VIOLET. I'll go.

ERNIE. It'll be the newspapers, let me. Wow – it's hotter than Calcutta.

(**ERNIE** *goes fast.* **CLEM** *looks around – a pause.*)

CLEM. (*To* **VIOLET.**) The beans are doing well. I must tie those tomatoes back. I think I'll elicit Mr Kerne to give me a hand sorting the garden for winter.

(*The phone starts to ring again.*)

VIOLET. Clem, you *must* change.

CLEM. (*He smiles.*) Did you hear they got word from their boy Archie? A letter. He says we won't know him when he gets back. Terrible being a POW, I'd imagine. What our people have been through.

VIOLET. Pull yourself together, Clem.

CLEM. This is going to be a heck of a thing, Vi.

>   *(He smiles.)*

The Treasury papers make miserable reading.

>   *(**VIOLET** embraces **CLEM**. She pulls back.)*

VIOLET. There's no one else.

CLEM. No. Probably not.

>   *(She breaks. **HERBERT** and **ELLEN** are there.
>   **CLEM** smiles, surprised.)*

Ellen, Herbert. Welcome. What are you doing here?
This morning?

HERBERT. We came up through the garden – there are a
couple of hacks out front.

ELLEN. We wanted to see you.

ERNIE. *(Returning.)* What about?

HERBERT. This won't take five minutes. We'd like to talk to
you alone. Please.

VIOLET. Ellen, you are always three moves ahead! That
hat. I probably should have tried to get something new
for the Palace. His Majesty will understand, I imagine.
Something of a surprise, after all.

ELLEN. Violet, this matters.

VIOLET. Oh, what I wear matters, don't you think?

HERBERT. Clem, we really would like a word. It's time to
face facts.

>   *(**CLEM** finally lights his pipe.)*

As you know, there are many in the party and the
unions…

ERNIE. Are there?

HERBERT. *(Tense.)* There are Ernie.

ERNIE. Not the unions, Sonny Jim. Not my people.

CLEM. Ellen, would you please keep Violet company? This all looks a horribly serious affair.

(He sets off towards the house.)

HERBERT. *(He needs* **ELLEN**.*)* Yes, but...

(The phone starts to ring again.)

CLEM. Oh, for a little P and Q!

ERNIE. *(Following* **CLEM**.*)* I'll answer. You better be snappy, Morrison; Mr Attlee has an appointment or two.

CLEM. *(Going.)* I gather it's quite a result. Your manifesto was brilliant, Herbert.

(Gone.)

VIOLET. Do you know, I really could not trust Clem at the wheel, so I drove him. Thousands of miles. Totnes all the way to Glasgow! In that little Austin. Quite a thing with fuel coupons! And those frightful hotels.

ELLEN. I think I should go and...

VIOLET. I voted for Mr Churchill. Do you know that? I've never been a socialist, and the communists absolutely freeze my blood – horrible people.

ELLEN. It's a free country.

VIOLET. It is, at the moment. Thank heavens.

ELLEN. I think...

VIOLET. *(Ignoring her, smiling.)* You've never wanted children of your own? You're probably asked all the time, aren't you? My calling was – and believe you me, it still comes as a surprise – to make a place for them:

the children, and Clem, to spring off from. I suppose for you, everyone is your child. The reason for your crusading, campaigning. For the sacrifices.

ELLEN. *(Laughs – not easy with this.)* I don't make sacrifices! And I never had the time. Or the inclination. I'm on the move, always.

VIOLET. And you want to change the world.

>   *(**ELLEN** looks at her.)*

Oh, you do. You all do. You, most of all, Ellen.

ELLEN. I am going to go in and see what is happening.

>   *(**VIOLET** touches **ELLEN**'s arm.)*

VIOLET. I know precisely why you and Herbert came here today. Be very careful, Ellen. Things can be so brutish in politics, particularly for women. I suppose I'd better find a hat.

>   *(**VIOLET** passes **CLEM** as he appears. He is purposeful and breezy.)*

Oh your collar – I'll find you a fresh collar.

CLEM. There it is...

>   *(Papers on the table.)*

My speech.

ERNIE. *(Following, urgent.)* The cars are here. The BBC are now calling it a landslide.

>   *(He goes. **CLEM** turns to **ELLEN**.)*

CLEM. Well.

>   *(The speech.)*

I rather convinced myself this would never be needed.

ELLEN. What do you think of what Herbert said, Clem?

CLEM. What Herbert said? Oh, that. Yes.

(He smiles.)

I am frightfully lucky. I grew up in a very nice home. An enchanted world. My school ran a club in Stepney. You know the sort of thing: "young men need to understand how the other half live..."

ELLEN. Clem, we must talk. I've always admired you, but I don't think this is the way forward.

CLEM. *(Ignoring her.)* ...that is something that *you* understand more than most. At eighteen, I volunteered to spend the summer teaching at the club. PE, cricket, anything I could do to be useful. The Stepney lads were thin as rakes and uncertain most of them. They were hard to trust but easy to care about. Thirty odds and sods, but, do you know Ellen, I realised I was happy being with them, helping them!

(He smiles.)

The Inns of Court or a solicitors office in Croydon weren't going to be for me. I learnt a thing or two there.

*(**HERBERT** has appeared. He stands watching.)*

Then along came the Great War.

ELLEN. You have led the Labour Party exceptionally for twelve years, but we do need a change, Clem.

CLEM. I enlisted: The King. The Country. Empire. Before going overseas, I got my ruffians together. We played a couple of good matches. I ended up in Gallipoli. It was unimaginable – all of it. But, again, I was lucky. I was injured. When the war was over, I had no idea what to do, so I went back to Stepney. I was determined to play cricket with the boys all the same. All but two of them were dead. Enlisted early. I will always wonder if they fought for King and country, or was it just warm clothes and a full meal? Rifle extra.

(**CLEM** *shakes his head.*)

CLEM. Seeing those two remaining boys, I decided.

(**ERNIE** *and* **VIOLET** *appear.*)

ERNIE. *(Loud.)* Clem, we are going to be late. For the Palace.

(**VIOLET** *touches* **ERNIE**'s *hand to stop him.*)

CLEM. From the moment those boys were conceived their destiny was set in stone. How could they escape? They were in a world that believed it was best to keep them firmly in their place. So, I decided to spend my life doing what little I could to change that world. There.

(*He turns to* **VIOLET**. *She takes his hand. They go.*)

ERNIE. You know, in France, with the peace, they've been knocking on doors. If they think you betrayed them, they say bonjour and shoot you in the face.

HERBERT. Oh fuck off, Ernie.

ERNIE. Herbert, you know I do sometimes wonder how you put up with us mere mortals.

(*To* **ELLEN**.*)* Oh, do smile, dear; you've just won us a one-hundred-and-forty-six-seat majority.

(**ERNIE** *goes, laughing.*)

HERBERT. *(An excuse.)* Christ, Clem is a slippery eel. I am going to ring around. I have support across the party.

ELLEN. You dithered.

HERBERT. What the hell is that supposed to mean? I should be Prime Minister.

ELLEN. Too late. It's what bullies do. Dither.

(*She stops herself, turns and limps away.*)

HERBERT. Where are you going?

ELLEN. Back to London.

HERBERT. My driver...

ELLEN. I'll walk.

HERBERT. It's twelve miles. What about your leg, Ellen?

ELLEN. I'll walk.

(**ELLEN** *goes.*)

Scene Six

(Number 10 Downing Street.)

*(**CLEM** is sitting working at the cabinet table. Red boxes, papers. It already feels like a lot of work. A cigar is in an ashtray. **JOAN** takes the papers once **CLEM** has signed them.)*

CLEM. *(Without looking up.)* Thank you.

(To himself.) Hmm.

(He jots notes.)

For the Foreign Office, yes?

*(He hands her a document. **ELLEN** appears. Stubborn, limping forward. **CLEM** doesn't look up from his work.)*

ELLEN. Clem.

*(**JOAN** is surprised by **ELLEN**'s determination.)*

JOAN. Prime Minister!

*(**CLEM** looks up, surprised.)*

CLEM. Do come in, Miss Wilkinson. Ah. You have.

*(**ELLEN** is about to speak when **CLEM** does.)*

Winston left his cigars everywhere. Miss...

ELLEN. Her name is Vincent. Joan.

*(To **JOAN**.)* Who'd have thought it, eh, lass?

JOAN. Thank you for putting a word in for me.

ELLEN. I didn't. Anyway, I doubt it would have done you much good.

(*To* **CLEM**, *about* **JOAN**.) Bright, this one. And not an old croc' like us.

> (**ELLEN** *laughs;* **JOAN** *is embarrassed.*)

CLEM. The infernal cigars. Would you, Miss Vincent, kindly.

JOAN. Sir.

> (**JOAN** *takes the cigar and ashtray.*)

ELLEN. (*Sniffing.*) Frankincense, myrrh, Clem – whose funeral?

CLEM. Ah. Who indeed. Now. Ah.

> (*He adjusts his glasses.*)

You do know if it hadn't been for you – people like you – we would still be appeasing Hitler? I have particularly fond memories of our time together in Madrid during the Spanish Civil War, you showed me...

ELLEN. Shut up, Clem, please.

> (*Slight pause.*)

Sorry, but you are wondering if I can be trusted?

> (**CLEM** *looks at her.*)

I didn't think you should be Prime Minister. No.

CLEM. Right.

ELLEN. I have worked all my life to see a Gov... to be part of a Government like OURS. I have campaigned. Not just with the Jarrow marchers, but my entire life, for social justice. You know the road we have been on. I cannot see this...this moment and not serve. You.

CLEM. Ellen...

ELLEN. There is so much to do. Look at us. Here, in power.

(*She smiles but is emotional and energized.*)

We can – you can – we can change everything. But we do need to act NOW. Want, Disease, Ignorance. Clem...

(*Again,* **ERNIE** *has appeared unnoticed – a shadowy figure.*)

ERNIE. But we have a country to run.

(**ELLEN** *turns to him, back to* **CLEM**. *She is closer to anger than self-pity, flying, and talking fast.*)

ELLEN. But even with our – the – your majority now, you've got to see, you're going to have to fight for every inch, and you know I can fight. I am one of the best fighters. 'Red Ellen'. My father was a strict man – a Methodist. And we were poor. We had next to nothing. But my father taught me to be rigorous. He was. About his God. About his principles and about his duty. I learnt from him – duty, certainty. Be certain of what you believe. You can't be half in, half out. Be certain. I can fight Clem, you know that.

ERNIE. The Prime Minister has a very full diary.

ELLEN. Don't make me beg. This is our prize. Don't make me beg Clem.

(*Finally, she stops.*)

CLEM. Prime Minister, if you don't mind.

(*He doesn't look at her. This is a horrid moment.* **JOAN** *appears.*)

JOAN. Prime Minister, the switchboard is ready. Sir.

(*She places a telephone on the table.*)

ERNIE. Miss Wilkinson. Dear.

> (**ELLEN** *nods, turns, and is walking away...*)

CLEM. Ellen. *Can* you be trusted?

ELLEN. You have to ask?

> (*She walks out into the wilderness.* **CLEM** *has a sheet of paper. He writes, looks at it, finally –*)

CLEM. Good. The Cabinet.

> (*He hands the paper to* **ERNIE**. *Stands.*)

ERNIE. Hugh Dalton to the Treasury. Grumpy bugger wanted the Foreign Office!

CLEM. I want you to be Foreign Secretary.

ERNIE. But I want to fight for my people. At home, Prime Minister.

CLEM. And I need you with me, against Stalin. You seem to understand him.

ERNIE. Is that meant to be flattering?

CLEM. And the Pacific War is still...well, terrible. The Japanese will not be easy. There is everything to do. And you know the world.

ERNIE. I am the illegitimate son of a farm labourer from Somerset.

CLEM. We all come from somewhere. Mr Bevin? Ernie?

ERNIE. I would be honoured.

CLEM. (*Smiling.*) I hope you will say that in a couple of years.

> (**ERNIE** *looks at the list.*)

ERNIE. Trade: Stafford Cripps. The man needs a proper meal. All that vegetarian nonsense. But right man, right job.

> (*Now he stops.*)

Morrison. As your deputy?!

CLEM. I gave him my word.

ERNIE. He is a devious schemer.

> (**CLEM** *looks levelly at* **ERNIE**.)

But, as you say, you gave him your word.

> (*He looks at the list. Frowns – alarmed.*)

Miss Wilkinson for Health?

CLEM. Foreign Secretary?

ERNIE. Obviously she was quite a campaigner, but... I do worry about Ellen – I worry about *her* health.

CLEM. None of us are in the first flush of youth!

ERNIE. Ellen and Herbert, Clem. There are rumours.

CLEM. What sort of rumours?

ERNIE. Rumour sort of rumours.

> (**ERNIE** *moves his hips – the shyest hint of sex.* **JOAN** *stares into the middle distance.*)

With all Herbert's plotting and conniving, I'd send a bunch of my dockers from Limehouse around to knock his teeth out if it were me.

CLEM. But Herbert *can* be in the Cabinet and Ellen *can't*? In my experience, scandals usually involve two people.

ERNIE. (*Direct.*) Ellen is too passionate, too emotional.

CLEM. When a moment ago she was too fragile? Could I...?

(He takes the paper from **ERNIE**, **CLEM** *writes.)*

Ellen understands the people. And she has friends in high places. Winston adores her. She's remarkable. And the Jewish refugees – she's been vital for them...

ERNIE. You are leaving her on the back benches not writing her obituary!

(To **CLEM**.) It is good to have a Prime Minister who listens. Mr Churchill would just push on. For Health and Housing, I do have a couple of...

*(***CLEM*** hands the papers back to* **ERNIE**.)*

ERNIE. *(Incredulous.)* Bevan: Health and Housing? Clem, you cannot do this...

CLEM. Prime Minister, if you please.

ERNIE. Aneurin Bevan is a rabble-rousing bully boy.

CLEM. But wouldn't he be *my* rabble-rousing bully boy? Nye Bevan Health. And Housing. And poor scandalous Ellen: Education, don't you think, Mr Bevin?

*(***ERNIE*** stares at* **CLEM** *– finally.)*

ERNIE. Prime Minister.

CLEM. Run this down to the typing pool, Miss Vincent, if you would.

*(***JOAN*** takes the document.)*

ERNIE. We weren't elected to put revolutionaries into Government.

CLEM. We were elected to change things. Wasn't that the general idea?

Scene Seven

(10 Downing Street.)

*(**CLEM** sits – telegrams in front of him.
VIOLET comes in in her dressing gown.)*

VIOLET. Clem, it's five thirty in the morning. You must get some sleep.

CLEM. "To see a World in a Grain of Sand

And a Heaven in a Wild Flower

Hold Infinity in the palm of your hand

And Eternity in an hour…"

I have had Blake with me – through the night.

*(He turns to **VIOLET**; he is ashen.)*

VIOLET. Let's find you some fresh tea.

*(**CLEM** starts to shiver.)*

CLEM. Oh. Shivers. Terrible.

VIOLET. I'll run you a hot bath.

CLEM. The war is over, Vi. The Japanese have surrendered.

*(But **CLEM** doesn't move or seem happy.)*

We have fought to save ourselves. What we have done was necessary – all of it.

VIOLET. This is exhaustion. Pull yourself together. That's the way.

*(She puts her arms around **CLEM**; they hold each other.)*

Let's get you ready for the bastards, shall we?

CLEM. You are describing His Majesty's Government.

VIOLET. I am certain the King and I are of the same mind. Better?

CLEM. Survivable. Thank you.

Scene Eight

(10 Downing Street.)

*(***ERNIE, HERBERT, HUGH DALTON, RICHARD STAFFORD CRIPPS** all hold papers. **STAFFORD** has an edgy fragility. **HUGH** is four square: tough, arrogant. **HERBERT** glances at his watch as...)*

ERNIE. *(Shouting.)* The fucking Yanks have done this because we are socialists!

HERBERT. *(Calm.)* Don't be absurd; the war is over. Everything was bound to change.

ERNIE. Truman instructing the fucking State Department to cut off *all* financial support to these islands was not *bound* to fucking happen, Herbert. Roosevelt would never have done...

HUGH. It may have escaped your notice but Roosevelt is dead.

STAFFORD. A frightful loss. To us all. To the world...

ERNIE. Not the fucking universe, Stafford?

*(***CLEM** comes in – holding papers.)*

CLEM. Morning.

(Off the papers.) Economics are not my strongest hand, but this all looks bleak. Hugh?

HUGH. Ernie, you know it would have been helpful to know what American thinking was going to be...

ERNIE. I am Foreign Secretary, not a fucking mind reader. *You* are the Chancellor of the Exchequer.

HUGH. Prime Minister, I am bound to warn you this is an extremely serious development. I wonder if the Foreign Secretary might change minds...

ERNIE. For pity's sake, Dalton!

STAFFORD. It is as big a crisis as Dunkirk. A financial Dunkirk!

ERNIE. Oh, stop being hysterical, Stafford.

STAFFORD. I am being realistic, Bevin. Our national debt is fifteen times our reserves.

HUGH. Sterling is under pressure...

STAFFORD. The country is in very real danger of going bankrupt.

ERNIE. Countries do not go bankrupt.

STAFFORD. If you say so.

ERNIE. *(Loud.)* You are Minister of Trade: increase fucking trade!

STAFFORD. It's not easy, you know...

HUGH. We have three million servicemen desperate to come home! The war has cost... Ernie, let me finish for once...and we have an Empire we simply cannot afford.

ERNIE. *(Shouting.)* The Empire is where our strength comes from.

STAFFORD. You say that to people when they are living on boiled potato soup with nettles.

ERNIE. Is that a vegetarian speciality?

STAFFORD. I need a glass of water.

HUGH. Three hundred million people in India, hundreds of millions more in Malaya, Burma and Ceylon, and the Palestine, Suez, Aden...

ERNIE. Truman is playing silly buggers. To think how we held out before Pearl Harbour...

HUGH. *(Continuing.)* ...a great proportion of the world, with the war over, depends on us.

STAFFORD. We simply cannot allow starvation like we did in India. Clem what Churchill allowed...

HUGH. We do not have the money to stop it!

STAFFORD. Please don't shout, Hugh. I'm sorry, but my nerves, Hugh...

ERNIE. BahBahBah. You are like a flock of bleating sheep.

> (*Finally*, **CLEM** *takes off his glasses and wipes them.*)

CLEM. And to think we won. The war and the election. All rather ironic, now, isn't it?

> (**HERBERT** *smiles and spots his moment.*)

HERBERT. (*Smooth.*) Prime Minister, we have only minutes before the full cabinet meeting. You will have read that what Mr Keynes is proposing...

> (*He holds out papers.*)

...in these pages. He is a very clever economist, you know. It is something really quite sophisticated.

> (**HUGH** *is about to interrupt.*)

Hugh, if *I* can explain – as I do grasp this.

> (**ERNIE** *rolls his eyes.*)

What Maynard Keynes is proposing is that we *borrow* to invest in the economy.

CLEM. Yes. Have I got this right? Borrow on top of the money we already have borrowed? A loan on top of a loan to pay off our debts?! Chancellor?

STAFFORD. Herbert, have you tried asking your bank manager for a 'loan on top of a loan to pay off a loan'?

*(Laughter, **HERBERT** glances at his watch.)*

HERBERT. *(Fast, serious.)* The key thing is to borrow to *invest*! Industry and factories. Rebuild the railways. Stimulate the economy. Growth. We will not only recover but flourish!

ERNIE. Go cap in hand to the Yanks, and they will want something in exchange! The Americans have a very different world in their sights. A world in which we are barely a shadow of our former selves!

(Big Ben starts to toll eight.)

CLEM. Gentleman – not for general consumption...

*(Before anyone is ready, **ELLEN** strides in – wearing a bright new coat. **JOAN** rushes in behind her. Everyone is surprised.)*

ELLEN. Meeting is at eight? Am I late?

CLEM. Sorry – er – Miss Vincent, would you be so kind as to ask Cabinet to wait five minutes.

*(To **ELLEN**.)* Minister, would you mind?

ELLEN. *(Smiling but going nowhere.)* What? What's afoot?

STAFFORD. Nothing. Heady stuff, really. Some of us are cursed to share the thin air around the PM.

HUGH. Just a pre-match chin wag.

*(But **ELLEN** goes to a chair and everyone stands.)*

CLEM. Good morning, Miss Wilkinson.

ELLEN. Please don't stand, Clem. We have a revolution to carry out. Churchill and his dogs will be at our heels...

CLEM. Let's not forget we were in Government with those 'dogs' a couple of months ago!

*(Then, **NYE** arrives from another door. He wears a smart brown suit – each suit marks a change in his status. He carries a box of papers.)*

NYE. ...which means we know what they eat and where they do their business! I am late, Mr Attlee. An unexploded German bomb at Victoria delayed my progress from Chelsea. And truth be told: I had no idea which was the Cabinet Room...

(He looks at the gathered.)

Has someone died?

*(**STAFFORD**, **ERNIE**, **HUGH** and **HERBERT** can barely contain their dislike of **NYE**.)*

CLEM. No, all in good health, thank you Mr Bevan.

ELLEN. *(Pushing.)* I thought once the war was over, we might do away with all that hush-hush-careless-talk-way of operating? As the Cabinet wait, this 'chin wag' is TOP secret?

*(A slight pause – the **MEN** don't know what to say.)*

HERBERT. Quite your colour – that coat.

ELLEN. Thank you, Mr Morrison, a trick I learnt from Her Majesty to catch the eye. Prime Minister, what were you talking about...?

*(**ERNIE** pulls a brown paper bag from his briefcase – changing the subject.)*

ERNIE. One of my lads in the Transport and General, had a word with the shop steward at Southampton Number 5 Pier on the QT. His cousin or father-in-law or summat got hold of these.

(The paper bag is full of bananas.)

HERBERT. *(Laughing.)* Is this a zoo?

ERNIE. Why we have an Empire! Enjoy it, boyo, this may be your last meal if Britain is bankrupt.

ELLEN. Bankrupt?

ERNIE. PM and I went to Potsdam immediately after the election. Mr Stalin was surprised that Churchill hadn't lined us all up against a wall and had us shot!

> *(Some laughter.)*

He was serious. Stalin and the hard Left in Europe are in cahoots. The war may be over, but nothing is settled...

> *(**NYE** is carefully handing out stapled papers to each person.)*

D'you mind, lad...?

NYE. You carry on, Ernie, don't you mind me.

ERNIE. I have been a Minister of State, Mr Bevan, for several years now.

NYE. Foreign Secretary, my apologies. You carry on...

> *(**NYE** continues putting papers in front of everyone.)*

ELLEN. The Leader in *The Times* reckons this Cabinet is a Communist cell! Prime Minister, please, if there is an economic issue...

CLEM. Thank you, Foreign Secretary. Sir Stafford Cripps. Your Ministry – Industry, Trade?

> *(**HUGH** gesture to **JOAN** – tea. She goes.)*

STAFFORD. Exhaustion. People. Machinery. Exhausted. And worse.

ERNIE. *Worse?* What is the matter with you, Stafford?

STAFFORD. *(Interrupting* **ERNIE**.*)* Exhaustion of raw materials! Steel, cotton, wood, and leather are in desperately short supply, and so where we have output or, rather, the capacity for output, we don't have the wherewithal.

CLEM. *(Turning to* **HUGH**.*)* Chancellor, lift our spirits.

STAFFORD. *(Continuing.)* I am sorry, Clem. I do really feel I have to be clear.

> *(He grins.)*

However, however, we will proceed with the nationalisation of both coal and steel. Continuing wartime controls will help, of course, but we cannot go back to low productivity and incompetent management. To solve this will take national will. Effort. And money, dare I...

HUGH. *(Dry, dogged.)* However much the Foreign Secretary wishes otherwise, this is a crisis.

ERNIE. You're a pessimistic type of bugger, aren't you, Hugh – always have been.

ELLEN. A crisis?

HUGH. I am a realist, Ernie. Is it that that sets us apart?

ELLEN. What is the crisis?

HERBERT. Dull economics, Miss Wilkinson.

ELLEN. Bore me.

> *(***JOAN*** returns with an industrial teapot.)*

HERBERT. Not yet, Miss... *(He can't remember her name.)*.

> *(***JOAN*** puts the teapot on the trolley.)*

STAFFORD. *(A whisper – he suffers from colitis.)* Oh no biscuits for me; they create havoc with my...you know.

ELLEN. I'm sorry, but *what* is the crisis? Mr Morrison?

STAFFORD. *(Whispering to **JOAN**.)* And black, when the time comes, if you don't mind, dairy is infernal. Thank you, though.

CLEM. Please, Stafford!

STAFFORD. I was talking to the tea girl, PM. Sorry. Shouldn't she serve? The girl.

ELLEN. Stafford, she has a name…

JOAN. *(Interrupting, embarrassed.)* That's alright, Miss Wilkinson.

ELLEN. But you do, Miss Vincent.

> *(She turns to **CLEM**.)*

PM…?

> *(**JOAN** puts biscuits on the table.)*

…if there is a crisis, the Cabinet should know?

> *(**HUGH** reaches for **STAFFORD**'s biscuit.)*

HUGH. As you don't want yours, do you mind?

ELLEN. Prime Minister, we have collective responsibility. Surely?

> *(**JOAN** gets tea cups and puts them on the table.)*

CLEM. This isn't quite what we hoped for. Things are, well, tiresome at best.

ELLEN. Clem the economy will influence what we can achieve, won't it?

CLEM. Always look forward, Miss Wilkinson, forward. Education?

(**ELLEN** *pauses – and decides to stop pushing.*)

ELLEN. I have to say I was bloody glad to leave school as a nipper, Prime Minister.

HUGH. Could you pass the sugar?

ELLEN. My fingers and toes used to freeze. Now, at a rough estimate, seventy percent of our schools are either dilapidated or damaged. Nothing has changed. I am conducting a survey of school buildings, and I will be bringing to Cabinet both proposals for repairs but also hundreds of new school buildings.

CLEM. We will look forward to your proposals with great interest.

ELLEN. A major building programme but a financial crisis will kibosh everything, won't it?

(*No reply.*)

And every child will be given a meal at school. Hunger is a silent scourge.

HUGH. There's a last biscuit, anyone?

(*He takes it.*)

HERBERT. Inspiring, very, Miss Wilkinson. Vital. Costly, though. Inspiring.

ELLEN. And, I propose we raise the school leaving age and change how we approach technical qualifications. Mr Butler's Education Act from the National Government will be a basis, but I am determined we go much further.

(**HERBERT** *looks to* **CLEM**. *He is looking at his pipe.*)

HERBERT. Laudable, also, but raising school leaving age will reduce our workforce...

ELLEN. Prime Minister, please...

STAFFORD. If, say, five hundred thousand youngsters stay in school for another year, that is five hundred thousand fewer workers building, repairing, farming. As Minister of Trade, that will keep me up at night.

HERBERT. *(Laughing.)* We can't afford half a million youngsters staring out the window as some poor teacher tries to drill something into their skulls!

ELLEN. Proper education is the basis of everything.

(Snapping.) Please don't shrug like that, Mr Morrison.

ERNIE. *(Laughing.)* She has a point – you do hold your genius in very high esteem, Herbert.

STAFFORD. Stalin may have been on to something with his shooting people, you know.

(Laughter.)

CLEM. Mr Bevan, you are unusually silent.

NYE. Not silent, Prime Minister, listening.

CLEM. And what did you hear?

NYE. Fear.

ERNIE. For pity's sake...

NYE. *(Ignoring **ERNIE**.)* Prime Minister, you have in front of you the National Health Service Bill.

ELLEN. The whole thing?

NYE. I want to take it to the House as soon as I have the Cabinet's approval, Prime Minister.

STAFFORD. *(Off the document, startled.)* "Complete Nationalisation of All Services"? Oh. Gosh.

ELLEN. *(Stunned.)* You've been working!

NYE. When you find a seam, it's best to work it hard and fast.

HERBERT. I should have opened a book on how long it would take Mr Bevan to get to mining and the pits. And the rain eh? The Welsh rain!

> *(He laughs, alone. Everyone reads, the clock ticks.)*

STAFFORD. *(Reading, startled.)* "...the Minister of Health will take over the full ownership of *all* hospitals, voluntary and municipal..."

HUGH. "Consultants will provide services not only in hospital but also at the patients' homes, where necessary..."

HERBERT. *(Standing.)* How many Harley Street consultants have you actually met, Mr Bevan?

STAFFORD. ...and all Health Centres, clinics, physiotherapists, *dentists* shall be free of charge."

NYE. There is little novel in the notion of proper health care for our citizens. Where my proposition – the pages you have in your hands, Prime Minister – differ from Mr Beveridge and his report – or the pre-war campaigns – it is my certainty that the most effective scheme will be one that is absolutely universal and supports every citizen as equals. Very simple, you see.

> *(He smiles.)*

In Tredegar, a small weekly compulsory contribution meant that every man, woman or child received the finest health care at the point of need. If they required hospitalisation, a taxi would take them...

STAFFORD. Tredegar is what, ten or eleven thousand people? Britain has a population of fifty million people...

HUGH. That's a lot of taxis.

NYE. The scale is different. The principle is the same. But we also saw how effective medical coordination was in large conurbations during the bombing.

HERBERT. Is that why you were tireless in Parliament criticising everything we did during the war?

CLEM. Happily, Mr Morrison, hostilities have now ceased.

HERBERT. This is all crazily too ambitious, Clem!

ELLEN. It was 'too ambitious' to put sanitation into deep shelters in the blitz! Experts said we'd be lucky to be started by 1968. Kick the right bums, and a couple of months later, hey presto!

HERBERT. With bombs dropping, I could run the three-minute mile!

ELLEN. No longer, no? So show Mr Bevan the courtesy of giving him a hearing, yes?

(**HERBERT** *is furious, but* **NYE** *pushes on.*)

NYE. There will be large regional health authorities coordinated by Central Government. We will take *all* hospitals into government management: Maternity homes, sanatoria, mental hospitals, you name it. All will be nationalised and run by the Ministry of Health. Consultants, doctors, nurses – the *entire* system of care will be managed by the state.

(*To* **STAFFORD** *who is searching.*)

Sir Stafford Cripps, page three. At the local level, we will have health centres that will offer General Practice, nursing as required, and be used, in case of emergencies, as central co-ordinators. Nothing to do with the care of our fellow citizens can be left to profiteering private companies.

HUGH. There is no way Britain can afford this.

STAFFORD. And we really cannot commit future generations to debt. I'm sorry, Prime Minister...

NYE. Nonsense. A fit population will make a strong and productive society. In Tredegar, people worked harder, knowing they had a safety net.

STAFFORD. Germany, *defeated* Germany, already has factories working properly less than a year after we defeated them. They already have output. We do not.

ELLEN. People voted for change in their millions.

HUGH. The press get a sniff that we are undermining the City, or sterling, they will rip us apart.

ELLEN. Which is why we have to act now. And they will anyway, Mr Dalton.

HERBERT. Local Authorities actually do quite well organising health care. In Greater London coordination has been mostly outstanding...

NYE. Have you visited a voluntary hospital recently? Nothing more than poorhouses stuffed with the sick...

HERBERT. Sure, then close them! Replace them with local hospitals. Prime Minister Mr Bevan is in danger of throwing the good out with the bad...

NYE. If the wealthy want to help the less fortunate, nothing stops our NHS accepting donations.

HERBERT. It's not like that!

ELLEN. *(Loud.)* The wealthy have one objective – to keep their wealth while our people can go hang...

NYE. ...or die in their wars!

HERBERT. *(To* **CLEM**.*)* Prime Minister, of course, as a Labour government, everyone in this room shares the same objectives but...

ELLEN. *(Replying to* **HERBERT**.*)* But do we share the same objectives? Really?

HERBERT. And what precisely is that supposed to mean?

ELLEN. I think you know perfectly well what I mean.

> *(***ELLEN** *moves.)*

You felt fear, is that what you said, Mr Bevan? In this room? It's certainly what I feel. Secrets, fear, and us bickering. What are we worried about? Tomorrow's newspapers? You – we – I – all know that the British press is mostly a mouthpiece for the right. We know they will attack us, so let them. What is there to fear?

We are used to being on the outside. And compare our fear to the fear that our people endure. A child wakes with a fever...

> *(***JOAN** *watches her.)*

The rich will telephone the doctor and pay guineas – but ordinary, working people? Will they have the money saved? If not, what?

HUGH. All I am saying, Miss Wilkinson, is that the Treasury anticipated something less ambitious...

HERBERT. This isn't ambitious – it's cuckoo land politics.

ELLEN. Actually, it is the first step to achieving a proper, fair, Britain.

NYE. And it is not 'ambitious'. It is the least that must happen.

STAFFORD. My dear boy, we could start by simply being practical...

NYE. Did you tell Churchill to be practical when he demanded more Spitfires?

STAFFORD. *(Surprised.)* Well, yes, of course. Of course, we did.

HERBERT. *(Interrupting, shouting.)* This is just ridiculous! Can we move on and get back to Keynes and the fuc...

(*He stops himself.*)

...economy, Prime Minister?

STAFFORD. Please don't shout...

ELLEN. Herbert – you do know you look like a frog, with your neck all swelling up, when you are angry?

(To everyone.) What Bevan is proposing is vital.

HERBERT. Prime Minister, please listen: for one thing, we don't even have the people, the nurses or the doctors.

ERNIE. We have an Empire of workers. Many of them would be happy to come here – to Britain – to help. As nurses and, what have you. In gratitude, even.

ELLEN. And we have nearly seventy thousand demobbed army doctors...

HERBERT. Who are good at pulling shrapnel out of some poor chap's backside but will run a mile confronted by anything female.

CLEM. The revolutionaries are at the gate. I wondered what you were thinking, Ernie.

ERNIE. It's crackers! To promise nearly fifty million people truly universal health care – 'cradle to the grave' – is crackers. We clearly cannot afford to do this.

NYE. Then, raise taxes. The rich can pay...

CLEM. Isn't that what is expected of us?

ELLEN. This may be the only chance we will get!

ERNIE. Go down to the steel mills, the rail yards, or talk with the demobbed lads, or the women. No, no, talk with the women. This is not about people like us. This is about ordinary people. My people. My mother died when I was... she suffered because she could not afford the doctor *and* to feed her children.

(*He starts to cry.*)

Excuse me. We have all lost and seen suffering.

(*He pulls himself together.*)

Prime Minister, wasn't the general idea that we change things?

(**HERBERT**, **HUGH** *and* **STAFFORD** *are horrified.*)

ELLEN. The Nazis have torn to shreds what it means to be human. We have seen that now. And now, the American bombs on Japan have shown just what the world might become. A civilised society... (*Nye's bill.*) ...is *our* answer. It's quite simple. Universal health care is a fundamental human right.

HERBERT. No one is saying it's not...

ELLEN. Unless I'm missing something, you are saying precisely that.

HERBERT. Just because we all want a gold-plated horse with a horn sticking out of its head doesn't mean, sadly, that unicorns actually exist, Ellen, please. For pity's sake. Realism.

ELLEN. (*Furious.*) Mr Morrison you seem to forgotten what – what...

(**ELLEN** *gasps, breathes, gasps again – an asthma attack. Everyone stares at her.*)

CLEM. Miss Wilkinson – can we give you some water?

ELLEN. (*Popping pills, gulping water.*) Oh no. I'm as fit as the proverbial, thank you.

(*She composes herself.*)

ELLEN. Prime Minister: things change. There are no certainties. Our election, this moment, is a rare thing. We know that. We must not compromise. We need to act now. Whatever Mr Morrison says.

CLEM. Thank you…

NYE. Imagine how strong our people will be if we can still the fear Miss Wilkinson describes!

> *(Everyone turns to him.)*

Imagine an end to desperation. And imagine simple things: free dentistry, opticians, maternity units, the feeling of calm that good, experienced advice is close at hand will give our people. Imagine practitioners whose doors opened without charge. Imagine lying in a hospital bed, knowing that the whole country was at your side, caring for you, ensuring you get the best treatment and the most up-to-date medicine. My friends, illness, accidents, even a feeling of despair: these are not 'bad luck'. No, these things happen to each and every one of us. It is the stuff of life. The fit and well can no more turn their backs on the less fortunate than we can turn our backs on ourselves. This is our purpose. We put up statues of our leaders. Every town and village throughout the land has memorials to our war dead, but, truly, the greatest test of us as a nation is how we treat the ill, the fragile, and those who do not share our good fortune. Imagine our people free from fear.

ELLEN. It's beautiful, don't you see?

CLEM. Yes, I do.

> *(Pause.)*

And to think today started so ghastly. Miss Vincent – would you apologise to the Cabinet and ask that they join us. Mr Bevan, you must take this to the House.

HERBERT. *(Deeply alarmed.)* Where you have a one-hundred-and-forty-six-seat majority!

CLEM. Yes, Herbert, so I do.

End Act One

ACT TWO

Scene Nine

(Dolphin Square. Winter 1947.)

*(**ELLEN** is in the kimono. She and **HERBERT** are in an embrace on a bed. She turns away.)*

HERBERT. What is it?

(He goes on stroking her.)

ELLEN. Stop that.

(Gentle.) I sometimes hate adultery.

HERBERT. We are socialists; it's expected of us.

(He kisses her neck. She stands. Gets a cigarette.)

I can get us a table tonight. By the river. He's got nifty with the rations. Says he's got veal.

ELLEN. I'm up to Sheffield, Herbert. And then Manchester. I've work to do. There's a LOT to do.

HERBERT. He's very discreet. Take the early train. What are you doing on Christmas Day?

ELLEN. My sisters. Why? What's Christmas Day got to do with the price of eggs?

*(**HERBERT** goes to his suit and takes out some pills.)*

Herbert?

HERBERT. Damned indigestion.

> *(Takes the pills with water.)*

Shall I get dressed?

> *(**ELLEN** nods, and he goes to his clothes.)*

What's changed?

ELLEN. Nothing. I don't know. Everything.

> *(**HERBERT** returns to her – and tenderly puts his hands on her shoulders.)*

HERBERT. *(Gentle, seductive.)* Don't you ever want more?

ELLEN. Watching you wolf down a black market veal chop by candlelight in a darkened corner? How could I possibly want more?

HERBERT. You are lonely.

ELLEN. Am I?

HERBERT. I think so.

ELLEN. But I wasn't lonely when we were fucking – you remember – with the V1 rockets whizzing over our heads.

HERBERT. I meant now.

ELLEN. Oh, I know what you meant. But don't worry. I am as happy as Larry. Got my job, this place. I never wanted little hands on my apron strings, like Violet, half a pace behind the PM, barely allowed to open her mouth.

HERBERT. I was only suggesting dinner, Ellen...

ELLEN. Or Jennie Lee – one of the brightest sparks in Parliament, and she is, as we speak, darning Nye Bevan's socks.

HERBERT. She has never darned anything in her life! Miss Lee is a very impressive backbencher – her work for the arts.

ELLEN. She has given over everything to support him.

HERBERT. They are very loyal to each other.

ELLEN. Which you seem to regard as some kind of perversion.

HERBERT. Stop, Ellen, please, I know this mood –

ELLEN. But what about Margaret? Convinced, her husband strides the corridors of power like a colossus while you are squirrelled away here in Dolphin Square?

(**HERBERT** *grabs his clothes.*)

HERBERT. I've told you, Margaret doesn't care. So long as we are not a scandal.

ELLEN. So a secretive veal chop is what?

HERBERT. I'm sorry, Ellen...

ELLEN. You are not sorry, Herbert. You want it both ways – like your socialism! A marriage that you can do what you like in; politics that can change depending which way the wind is blowing.

HERBERT. We are too old for this.

(*Gentler.*) It's just that I sometimes think of you alone on Christmas Day. For one example.

ELLEN. Oh? While you and your little brood gather around Papa as you roast chestnuts on the fire and sip sherry?

(**HERBERT** *grabs his clothes and doesn't notice* **ELLEN** *gasping for breath.* **HERBERT** *is buttoning his shirt, his back to her.*)

HERBERT. I can't understand why you turn like this. It's unpleasant.

ELLEN. *(Gasping for breath.)* It – may – be – what – I – actually – think.

> (**ELLEN** *slides onto her knees, gasping.* **HERBERT** *turns, horrified.)*

HERBERT. Ellen?

> *(This is a severe attack.)*

What's wrong? Should I call someone? Who should I...

> (**ELLEN** *crawls across the floor, gasping, pointing at a chrome-plated nebuliser beside the bed.)*

OK. Ellen? Christ, this? Is this it?

> (**ELLEN** *gasps – and nods. He hands her the nebuliser – she breathes hard.)*

I'll fetch someone.

> (**ELLEN** *gasps – in out. Finally:)*

ELLEN. What are you going to do? Hide in the wardrobe?

HERBERT. I would *never* have done that.

ELLEN. I certainly would if you were dying on the floor!

HERBERT. Ellen, you need to see a doctor.

> *(He kneels in front of her.)*

ELLEN. A doctor? The press would destroy me – "Female minister not up to the job."

> *(They are physically close – she is still fragile but pulls away –)*

We are failing. It's a bloody mess, this government.

HERBERT. You are not well.

ELLEN. *(Interrupting, she pulls herself up.)* I want to get the job done, Herbert. That's all. We used to work eighteen-hour days, you remember? We never stopped.

HERBERT. It was the middle of the fucking war.

ELLEN. *(Shouting.)* But now? But now? You've forgotten. You've all forgotten. Nothing has changed. Two years in and nothing is getting done. It's the middle of winter and the wind is blowing through my schools like bloody sieves. And I haven't got enough teachers by a factor of about ten. What is the matter with you? Not just you – all of us? People are desperate for a roof over their heads, but spivs and Tory crooks are having a field day. All you are worried about, it seems to me, is your position so that when, *if*, Clem is in trouble, everyone will turn to you first.

HERBERT. I have no idea what's got into you.

ELLEN. Oh really, Herbert.

HERBERT. *(Stung.)* Go on – go to Manchester. Shove a couple of classes into Nissen Huts and keep the poor buggers trapped in school for another year. At least you can be confident: generations of bored school children will never forget you.

ELLEN. I don't want to be remembered. I want to make a difference.

HERBERT. How fucking pious. You know what your trouble is, you and Bevan; you both believe the world will change because you have decided it *must* change.

ELLEN. *(Emotional.)* Do you know what I think?

HERBERT. Ellen, please, let's start again. I'm sorry.

ELLEN. *(Ignoring* **HERBERT***'s apology.)* I think you are a coward.

HERBERT. A bully *and* a coward, now?! Wow. Ellen, I have fought...

ELLEN. You have jockeyed, you have manoeuvred, but how very fucking disappointing: you missed!

HERBERT. Ah – so this is what this is about? Still?

ELLEN. No. No, actually, it's not.

> *(They both hang there. Whatever is said next could be terminal. **HERBERT** turns away and finishes dressing. Finally, he speaks.)*

HERBERT. Maybe you should be less emotional.

ELLEN. What has emotion got to do with it?!

HERBERT. It confuses you.

> *(She stares at him, almost beyond anger.)*

Please can you check the landing? I don't trust those porters.

ELLEN. So, no table by 'the river'? All sotto voce. Just you slithering away down the service stairs? Or have I gotten all confused about that, too? Giddy with emotion.

HERBERT. You know what I mean.

ELLEN. Do I?

HERBERT. Shall I telephone a doctor before I go?

ELLEN. There's nothing wrong with me. Nothing. I have work to do. I'm off to Manchester. You go back to Westminster or wherever you are off to now, Herbert. How about home? The loving embrace of an eternally betrayed wife?

HERBERT. *(Firm.)* Can you check for me? The stairs.

ELLEN. No. I quite fancy a SEX scandal. Cheer the poor nation up. Everyone's miserable. We've won the war, but rationing is back. No more flying bombs, but EVERYTHING is still broken. There is one downside to a scandal when I think of it, isn't there: you'd lose your driver, eh Herbert? No, you get out of here, Herbert. Take the risk; go on. You never know what will happen if you go through that door. Maybe a porter. Maybe not. Maybe he'll sell our story for five guineas, maybe not.

(She smiles but is still enraged.)

Go on, Herbert, take a risk!

Scene Ten

(A club in Pall Mall.)

(Oil paintings. Immaculate tables. **WAITERS** *hover.* **LORD MORAN** *sits at one table.* **NYE,** *in another, smarter suit, stands.)*

MORAN. Pall Mall clubs' raison d'être is so that men like us can keep the world turning without anyone much noticing – Secretary of State.

(He indicates a seat.)

Sit, Mr Bevan.

NYE. You asked me to meet.

MORAN. I invited you to dinner.

NYE. Lord Moran, you are President of the Royal College of Physicians. The Royal Colleges and the British Medical Association are blocking my proposals. You are blocking His Majesty's Government...

MORAN. *(Oh come on.)* His Majesty!

NYE. ...and heading for a very difficult confrontation.

MORAN. As Mr Churchill's physician, I was with him the day he lost the election. He wept.

NYE. He knew his time was up.

MORAN. He felt he had let the British people down.

NYE. Not *my* people, Lord Moran. And besides, what does Mr Churchill have to do with anything now?

MORAN. Call me Charlie, do, please. Under the Lord this, or that, we are – most of us – human beings. Charlie, Nye, no?

(A **WAITER** *arrives with a trolly and starts serving fish for* **MORAN**.*)*

I have it on good advice that this fish is spectacular.

(*About the* **WAITER**.) Stubbs seems to know lots of lorries and has a marvellous aptitude for catching things – fish, French cheeses and such like – when they fall off the back of the aforementioned. Oh, at least drink with me...

NYE. Is the wine black market, too, Lord Moran?

MORAN. (*Laughing.*) God no! Do you know, they evacuated the entire cellar here to somewhere I dare think in the Welsh hills to save German wine from German bombs! Have you done the Moselle? The scent of earth and vineyards mingles with the cool air from the river.

NYE. Back-breaking work picking those grapes. What did you want to say?

(**MORAN** *looks at* **NYE**.)

MORAN. I like to think of myself as a caring but dispassionate intermediary between the world at large and your ideas...

NYE. The Labour Party's ideas. The ideas that millions of people in the country voted for.

(**NYE** *sits.* **MORAN** *holds up the Labour Manifesto and smiles.*)

MORAN. Did you write this? All this about good food, houses, and health centres and that "parenthood must not be penalised if the population of Britain is to be prevented from dwindling." It reads like a Government instruction to fornicate.

(*He laughs.*)

But it hardly is announcing to the British people that you intend to entirely and radically overhaul everything about their medical care...

NYE. I want to change a system that works for you.

MORAN. My profession.

NYE. But not those you serve.

MORAN. But politically...

NYE. Lord Moran, I don't need a lecture on politics. I have had human faeces posted through my letter box.

MORAN. Ghastly. Hot-headed young medics do get rather blasé about body parts and human waste.

NYE. My wife...

MORAN. I am sorry, but I'm sure she took it all in her stride. Quite a marriage, I am told.

NYE. My wife, my marriage, has nothing to do with this.

MORAN. Politics can become very personal, Minister.

NYE. Your colleagues remind me of militant jellyfish, if I'm honest. Lord above, imagine the first thing a baby sees on being born – one of those grey-faced misery guts staring down at his privileged little face!

    (**MORAN** *laughs;* **NYE** *is surprised.*)

All I am trying to do is fulfil a promise.

MORAN. So, will you force us to treat patients at the point of a gun? Fixed bayonets?

NYE. That is inane. We will pay doctors, of course. And pay the hospitals...

MORAN. And every general practice? Do you know how many of them are family businesses? Handed down father to son...

NYE. And that is supposed to inspire confidence? GPs will be in Community Health Centres. Every town and village will have one. Quick, easy access to care is fundamental. Now, I am busy, very, and it's late, so if you'll excuse me.

MORAN. I am trying to help you, for Christ's sake, man.

NYE. Then get your members to accept the inevitable.

MORAN. May I tell you what you face?

NYE. Over a year into this, I think I know.

MORAN. Why should my members lose what they have? They are learned men and women, dedicated and caring. They earn well…

NYE. You consultants run your own private fiefdoms, charging what you like. Nurses bow and scrape – while they do the bulk of the care. The system is class-riddled, hierarchical, and it's a bloody lottery how you get treated. We come from such different circumstances. When you fret about 'losing', I wonder, do you have any idea? I think you cannot imagine – you may see, but can you imagine? – the poverty, the desperation of so many of our countrymen and women?

MORAN. *(Firm.)* I am a doctor; I know suffering. I understand it. And if only you'd hear me, I am trying to find a solution.

> (**NYE** *toys with a glass.*)

Is that a new suit, Mr Bevan?

> (*He smiles, moving on.*)

I gather you're getting somewhere with the Nurses? But the dentists? The hip and knee boys? Paediatricians? Anaesthetists? Shall I go on? Pharmaceuticals, the makers of wooden legs, and glass eyes? Are you going to bully and cajole the whole shooting match?

> (**MORAN** *indicates the waiter who fills* **NYE**'s *glass.*)

NYE. I am. The system stinks. And you know it stinks. Teaching hospitals run by cabals. Rotten GPs. Terrible doctors making a tidy living handing their lists on to their gormless sons or selling them. Too many of them are charlatans who grudgingly, sometimes, accept a hock of ham or some other favour offered in desperation to misdiagnose...

MORAN. That suit is exceptional fabric.

NYE. Yes. My wife chose it.

MORAN. And very hard to come by, I am certain. She's right: a Minister in His Majesty's Government must dress the part, at least.

NYE. And now I reckon you are insulting both me AND my wife?

MORAN. Oh no: if I were to insult either of you, you would be in no doubt.

(Beat.)

Come on, taste it. Taste the wine. My dear chap – you must realise we see the direction of the tide, Minister. We just want to ensure nothing vital gets broken as it comes in and goes out.

*(**NYE** drinks.)*

That wine is made by God, don't you think, Mr Bevan?

Scene Eleven

(Railway stations – and a hospital in Birmingham.)

(Steam fills the stage. **ELLEN** *wears a coat and hat. She carries a case. People bump into her. Umbrellas, luggage. The thump-thump-thump noise again. The echo of a station tannoy. Then, out of the steam and the noise, a white enamel hospital bed hurtles downstage instead of a train.* **ELLEN** *is on the bed.)*

(A **SENIOR NURSE**, *an oxygen bottle and a medical trolley.* **ELLEN** *pulls herself upright. A* **DOCTOR** *in a white coat injects her.* **ELLEN** *slumps and then rises again.)*

ELLEN. *(Fighting.)* Please, I need my things, I need my clothes...

(The medication takes over, and **ELLEN** *slumps. The* **DOCTOR** *disappears. The* **SENIOR NURSE** *folds* **ELLEN***'s clothes and tidies her possessions.* **ELLEN** *stirs – very drugged – fighting it.)*

Where am I?

*(***ELLEN** *twists. There are shadowy figures everywhere; it is a drugged nightmare moment.)*

Who's there?! Who's there?! What do you want?

(She turns – **HERBERT** *– in hat and coat – moves towards* **ELLEN**.*)*

Herbert? What are you on earth are you doing here?

HERBERT. *(Whispers.)* I've settled up.

ELLEN. Herbert?

HERBERT. I paid. It's alright. And I gave a false name.

ELLEN. Please, Herbert, get me back to London. I need to...

> *(She pulls herself up.)*

I am not at my most ravishing, my darling, I do know, but this is ridiculous – a turn – my chest, nothing serious. I'll scrub up.

HERBERT. Ellen, you collapsed on the train.

ELLEN. What do you mean? Where am I?

HERBERT. Birmingham. The General Hospital. They stopped the Express from Crewe. Someone alerted the Guard. You are not well.

ELLEN. Who knows? How did you know? If this gets into the press...

HERBERT. The Sister will chase off any curious journalists; you are safely off the main ward. I don't think anyone knows who you are.

ELLEN. I need my things. Have you got your driver?

HERBERT. I heard, and I thought I...

ELLEN. But who told *you*? Herbert, please, you know what they will do to me. The papers will have a field day! Help me get up. Come on, help me.

> **(HERBERT** *is uneasy.)*

HERBERT. Actually, I am taking Margaret and Mary to the ballet. At Sadlers Wells. I came because...

ELLEN. You came to Birmingham to tell me you are going to the ballet?

HERBERT. Yes. I felt I really ought.

ELLEN. You *ought* to take me back to London.

> (**ELLEN** *looks at him. She tries to breathe.*)

Get me back to Dolphin Square, please. That's all I need…

HERBERT. It's my wife and daughter, Ellen – you have to understand.

ELLEN. Understand, sure. As long as we are not a scandal. I get it – can you imagine? I might drag you down. Sick – scandalously sick – the world will talk. Who was she with? On that train? In that hospital bed? I'm just a bit under the weather, Herbert.

HERBERT. I'm sorry, Ellen.

> (*Neither* **HERBERT** *nor* **ELLEN** *notice* **MORAN** *come in.*)

ELLEN. It was nothing. Us.

HERBERT. Ellen?

ELLEN. Nothing.

> (**MORAN** *clears his throat, and* **HERBERT** *turns – alarmed.*)

HERBERT. Miss Wilkinson we all, the Cabinet, wish you a full recovery. The Prime Minister says do take your time.

ELLEN. How kind.

> (**HERBERT** *passes* **MORAN**.)

HERBERT. Lord Moran.

MORAN. (*Smiling.*) Who'd have thought it: Herbert Morrison!

> (**HERBERT** *goes.* **MORAN** *takes* **ELLEN**'s *wrist and puts a stethoscope on her chest.*)

ELLEN. *(Quietly.)* Charlie? What are you doing here?

MORAN. I'm a doctor.

ELLEN. *(Pulling herself up.)* I have to get on my feet – I am giving a talk this evening in Holborn, and I am opening a new school hall in Bermondsey in the morning...

MORAN. Your heart is like a tiny bird exhausted after a terribly long flight, my dear. You've been asleep for nearly thirty-six hours. You are quite exhausted.

ELLEN. I've been so busy I just forgot to eat...

MORAN. How many of these things have you been taking? Daily? More than daily?

    (He holds up a bottle of pills.)

ELLEN. Those aren't mine.

MORAN. Ellen, please. Sister found them. In your handbag.

ELLEN. *(Cutting in.)* I have asthma.

MORAN. You have severe airway fibrosis from your asthma – not helped by your dedication to nicotine – that you have been 'treating' with amphetamines. Who is prescribing these? Some back street quack? This needs to stop – entirely. Would you like some water?

ELLEN. I want a couple of those pills t'be honest. Why on earth did you come? There are good doctors in Birmingham, aren't there? I need my damn clothes. I am fine...

MORAN. Winston asked me to.

ELLEN. Winston? What do you mean, Winston?

MORAN. He thinks highly of you.

    (He smiles.)

He thinks that deep inside, you are one of us.

ELLEN. He's wrong.

(A new idea.)

Charlie, you kept the boss going through the war, didn't you? Help me? Please – what did you give Winston? I need your help, just a little bit of something...

MORAN. Mr Churchill is a law unto himself.

(Change.)

Ellen, you are remarkable, really. What you have achieved!

ELLEN. Bloody hokum...

MORAN. And you have had more than your fair share of adventures, but now, most honestly, my dear girl, you have lived your life.

ELLEN. I'll be damned if I know what you are talking about. I'm not finished. If I shut my eyes – do you know what I see? Injustice.

MORAN. Ellen...

ELLEN. Not a word on a page, or even carved in granite...

(Gasping for air.)

...or talked about in Parliament or on the radio. No, I see them – the desperate, the poor, the starving...

(Gasping.)

...staring at me. I can't pass them by. It has been like that since before I can rem-e-mber. Winston is wr...

(She's struggling.)

MORAN. Oxygen.

(He reaches for the mask.)

ELLEN. Please, Charlie, just help me!

MORAN. Breathe – calm yourself. In – out – in.

> (**MORAN** *holds the oxygen over* **ELLEN**'s *mouth.*)

Do you seriously believe an industrialised health service could contain *you* or, for that matter, Winston? Or the rest of you? You can't be processed by Mr Bevan in his health factory. Your friend wants to turn us all into a grim department of Government. Corridors of bureaucrats and bean counters, but every patient, every doctor, is different. Sure, let's help the poor, but...

> (*Presses the mask on her face.*)

Ellen, there: in – out – in – out. It's just a journey. The beginning is bloody and dangerous – we are so lucky to get born alive... and at the end the best we can hope for is the easiest way out. And in between? For doctors, nurses, hospitals – our 'science' – is to nudge you this way and that. Not a service. Each patient is something different.

ELLEN. *(Fighting.)* No, I – have – to – we have a ch–

MORAN. Take a few days. Go to Switzerland. The Alps. Rest. You can afford that. Enjoy the time you have left.

ELLEN. Please I – need – to...

Scene Twelve

(10 Downing Street.)

(It is bitterly cold. Snow swirls. **JOAN** *appears, wheeling her bike.* **NYE** *comes fast from the other direction.)*

JOAN. Mr Bevan, you are very early?

NYE. I was summoned.

JOAN. Oh?

NYE. You don't know?

JOAN. No?

NYE. Oh just a chinwag, my best guess. Nothing important.

JOAN. No. Go in – I'll just put this in the Chancellor's yard.

(She wheels the bike away as **NYE** *goes into Number 10.)*

(The table. A brown enamel teapot, and dirty cups on a trolley. Alone, **NYE** *looks around. The clock ticks, and then, suddenly,* **ELLEN** *bowls in. She is weaker and wrapped up in a coat with a scarf around her head.)*

ELLEN. Morning, Nye.

NYE. Ellen?

ELLEN. Nye?

NYE. *(Conclusive.)* Ah.

ELLEN. *(The same.)* Ah. Something afoot, Minister?

*(***JOAN** *comes in, she stops, surprised to see* **ELLEN.***)*

JOAN. Miss Wilkinson? We heard that you were ill.

ELLEN. Been skiing in Switzerland. And I climbed the Matterhorn. Is the BBC now issuing hourly bulletins on my health? Where is everyone? The Cabinet should be meeting.

JOAN. It's not even seven.

ELLEN. *(Confused – laughing.)* Is that right? Crikey.

> *(She gasps. **JOAN** goes to her.)*

Leave be – do you hear me? Just...

> *(Determined recovery.)*

Well, give me the damn papers. I can get started, at least.

NYE. *(Changing the subject.)* One of the girls downstairs has a bar-fire literally under her chair. If someone doesn't get burnt to death, it will be a miracle.

JOAN. I'll read the riot act, Minister.

> *(**JOAN** prepares the room, **NYE** waits. **ELLEN** sits working through the cabinet papers. She's driven: scratching things out, scribbling fast. Finally...)*

NYE. Who wants breakfast?

> *(He holds out a bar of American chocolate to **JOAN**.)*

JOAN. It's delicious.

NYE. Friends in high places.

JOAN. Black market?

NYE. *(Laughing.)* Too late, you are a wicked woman. You've eaten it now.

ELLEN. Mr Bevan, I thought you were presenting your housing policy White Paper? These pages are thin reading.

NYE. Housing policy is in the garage – getting an oil change. There are obstacles. And I have been busy with the medical establishment, Ellen.

ELLEN. *(Easy.)* If the rumours are true, so have I.

(*He holds out the chocolate.*)

NYE. Ellen?

ELLEN. Keeping well, Nye? How's Jennie?

NYE. Scottish – she has a lower thermostat.

(*They eat the chocolate. There's a moment of ease between them.*)

ELLEN. Heaven. "As welcome as a fox in a hen house." Do you remember Nye? We were Clem's insurgents – how they tried to keep everything from us.

NYE. I still am an insurgent.

ELLEN. *(Laughing.)* "But there are obstacles." We should be fighting on.

NYE. And schools? How is *your* revolution?

(**ELLEN** *smiles – touché. She turns to* **JOAN**.)

ELLEN. What about you, Joan?

JOAN. Me? I'm so cold, honestly, I'm not sure who I am anymore.

ELLEN. It is colder than bloody Russia, and I have been there. The coldest winter in living etcetera. No romance in your life?

JOAN. In this weather? Anyway, far too busy for all that. My dad said "No time, child, for carry on. We got to make our way."

(She blushes, feeling she has over-shared.)

JOAN. I hope you don't mind me saying, but you should know: when we heard that you were ill...

ELLEN. *(Laughing, exasperated.)* Me ill? I had *completely* forgotten. But I was asking about *you*. You should not trudge through life alone, whatever your father tells you. We've not spoken, have we, properly? You are so young...

> *(**JOAN** is embarrassed. **ELLEN** takes her hand.)*

You are with the foxes now. You are filled with promise! Tell us your story. Where have you come from? What will you be?

NYE. *(A warning.)* Ellen, I think...

JOAN. I don't think I have a story. Really.

ELLEN. Your father?

JOAN. *(Now fighting emotion.)* A good man, Miss Wilkinson. And my mother. On my heart.

NYE. *(Changing the subject.)* You have been doing broadcasts, Ellen, yes, from Broadcasting House?

ELLEN. I'm sure you are making your family proud...

NYE. Time heals. Isn't that what they say, Joan?

> *(**ELLEN** is mystified. **HUGH** appears but stops upon seeing **ELLEN**.)*

HUGH. Ah.

ELLEN. You weren't expecting me? Lovely morning.

> *(**STAFFORD** and **HERBERT** come in. They are in gloves. **STAFFORD** has a scarf wrapped around his head. They both stop, seeing **ELLEN**.)*

STAFFORD. *(Displacement.)* Oh. There's no coal!

JOAN. PM says with the country having to ration coal, Downing Street should lead by example.

HUGH. How noble.

HERBERT. *(To* **JOAN**.*)* Rustle up the tea, can you, Miss…?

> (**HERBERT** *can't remember* **JOAN**'s *name, but* **STAFFORD** *indicates the trolly.* **HERBERT** *snaps.)*

Or do something, somewhere for crying out loud…

JOAN. *(Rattled.)* Mr Morrison.

NYE. Herbert, pick on someone your own size. And don't be a bloody arse.

> (**JOAN** *goes.* **HERBERT** *breathes heavily.* **NYE** *paces.)*

STAFFORD. *(Lifting the mood.)* Bevan, have you mugged one of your quacks for some of their keep-you-up-all-night pills?

NYE. According to the Daily Sketch, I'm a Nazi. Given me a lust for blood. What's this about?

HERBERT. Been in the wars, Miss Wilkinson? Poor you.

ELLEN. The tea's cold, or I'd be mother.

> (**HERBERT** *sits.)*

Herbert, you look like a dead fish. What are you lads up to?

> (*She stares at them – she is not going anywhere. This is decisive.)*

STAFFORD. Clem – the poor man – is really very unwell.

HUGH. The PM has a fever.

STAFFORD. I do fear it is something worse.

HUGH. He went on the BBC, telling everyone to pull together and put on their warmest jumpers.

NYE. Snow melts; it's not the end of the world.

STAFFORD. We are facing another financial crisis.

NYE. Not another one?

HUGH. Not something to laugh about! Exports are stopped dead. The docks are either frozen solid or deserted. And then there's the issue of convertibility. Do you know what that even means?

NYE. I have read the budget and study what the City of London says and conclude that most of what's amok in Britain is piss awful, selfish and short-term mismanagement. Excuse my language, Ellen.

ELLEN. I can handle a bit of piss.

(*To* **HUGH** *and* **STAFFORD**.) He's right. And Herbert wants to challenge Clem. And he wants you at his side.

NYE. I can see that.

ELLEN. You bloody well know that this is the wrong moment, Herbert...

HERBERT. This is the last fucking moment, Ellen!

ELLEN. A leadership contest will play right into Tory hands. Fleet Street will have a field day.

(**ERNIE** *appears in his big coat.*)

ERNIE. You plotting?

HERBERT. We need a new leader, Ernie. Absolutely.

HUGH. We are fighting for our lives. The economy is...

STAFFORD. Things are truly dire, Ernie. If we don't trade...

HERBERT. India is a blood bath, Ernie. And Palestine – ghastly business. You know we are in trouble abroad and at…

ERNIE. I am the fucking Foreign Secretary; I do have the vaguest idea of what is going on.

STAFFORD. And there are strikes! We are a Labour Government facing strikes. Right now, the trains don't even run…

ELLEN. Because of the snow!

ERNIE. You call a bunch of communist agitators refusing to go to work a proper strike? From memory, the last bastard who claimed to get the trains to run on time ended up hanging upside down from a lamp post in Milan.

HUGH. In the summer we are going to see a serious devaluation in sterling. It is the direct result of our arrangement with the United States. Our loan? When this happens – this –

(He holds a pound note.)

It will be worth half what it is now.

STAFFORD. Everything we import – oil, wheat, cotton, technology – everything that this island depends on will double in price. And whether we like it or not our imports rather dominate and our exports…

NYE. We are surrounded by cod, standing on coal. We'll survive.

HUGH. On our knees, Mr Bevan. On our damn knees.

HERBERT. I should lead the Government.

ERNIE. So, let's tear this Government to pieces because the weather's vile, yes?

*(Direct to **HERBERT**.)* Herbert, you aren't cut out to lead. Never were. Is that settled, lad?

HERBERT. I am sick of this. And you. I understand the economy, Bevin…

ERNIE. *(Ignoring* **HERBERT**.*)* Sir Stafford Cripps, Richard, what about you?

STAFFORD. *(He would.)* Me? Gosh, I…

ERNIE. *(Dismissive, mocking.)* "Me? Gosh."

STAFFORD. Ernie, you are an absolute brute, sometimes. Really.

ERNIE. Ellen, dear? What about you?

HERBERT. Oh, don't be absurd.

ELLEN. I do not want to, Ernie. But many thanks all the same.

ERNIE. *(Interrupting.)* Hugh? You are a cool head and can cut throats if required but I can't see you as Prime Minister, can you?

HUGH. I have always thought that I…

ERNIE. I think not. Don't you?

> *(***ERNIE*** smiles.)*

Do you know what shocks me most? You all seem to think that you change Mr Attlee for…

> *(Who?)*

And it will make a difference? This isn't about us. It never has been. We were lucky. The war and we were on the winning side…

STAFFORD. That we won. No question.

ERNIE. So we keep telling ourselves. We wouldn't have lasted after 1941 without the Yanks. Without the Dominions? Without the *Russians*? Listen to me, Herbert. And it isn't just about the war. We know what it was like before. We lost election after election. And let me say something else. This is probably the only chance we will get. This is our moment. And it will end. The people will tire of us; we will let them down, but now? Because of a few blizzards and trains stopped, and docks frozen, now? Change leader now?

HUGH. *(Strong.)* Bevin – you know we cannot go on like this. Clem does not understand economics at all.

ERNIE. Which is why you are his Chancellor. He doesn't understand Trade Unions, which is why he has me. For Industry: he has Stafford.

STAFFORD. Yes, Industry and Trade, Ernie.

ERNIE. Oh do shut up. That is why we are here. Now do your damn jobs.

> (**ERNIE** *looks at them and smiles hugely.*)

And then there's Aneurin Bevan. Everyone in the country knows who Mr Bevan is, don't they? You are a winner. You are whipping the entire medical industry into a frenzy, and do you know I reckon something? You will win, I think.

NYE. The Tories vote against us at every stage. They are effective...

ERNIE. But you will win.

NYE. I will.

ERNIE. Which is a good thing if you want to be Prime Minister. Do you want to be Prime Minister?

ELLEN. Nye?

HERBERT. Ernie, Nye...

ERNIE. Shut up, Herbert, you are ill.

HERBERT. He's too far left.

ERNIE. Now? Oh, Nye's quite the darling in Clubland these days. The good Lord Moran and others are lubricating your way, are they not? Did you *honestly* think that storming around smashing heads together was going to work? Every middle-class family has a medic somewhere close to its heart, and there's not a little girl who doesn't want to grow up to be a nurse. You go at them directly, and they will destroy you. Without Mr Attlee – eliciting Mr Churchill, who persuaded Moran to put his shoulder to your particular wheel – you would be nowhere.

ELLEN. Nye – say it!

> (**VIOLET** *follows* **CLEM** *as he comes downstage. He is in his suit but wears slippers and a blanket over his shoulders. He is grey, sweating, sick.*)

This is not right. We don't need change. We need to get on.

NYE. Our work isn't half done.

ELLEN. But betray Clem?

ERNIE. One last chance, Mr Bevan?

ELLEN. (*Smarting.*) Nye? The cock crowed three times, and he was silent...

> (*No one speaks;* **CLEM** *and* **VIOLET** *get closer.*)

CLEM. (*He's very fragile.*) Glorious morning. Good to see everyone. Keeping warm, Miss Wilkinson? I hear you've been under the weather somewhat.

VIOLET. The PM should be in bed. Clem, for pity's sake: stop.

CLEM. Kind. But no. The agenda – we must push on, don't we think?

VIOLET. Ernie, please?

(**ERNIE** *doesn't respond.*)

CLEM. Best foot forward.

(**CLEM** *reaches to* **VIOLET**. *She looks at him.*)

VIOLET. Does it matter this much? Look at you. Look.

CLEM. Yes, yes, it does.

VIOLET. It will kill you.

CLEM. Not yet it won't.

Scene Thirteen

(Nye and Jennie's home. Cliveden Place, Chelsea.)

(A complete change. Fun and laughter. There is a sofa. There is a wheeled table with a large covered object on it. A record plays – Charlie Parker's "A Night in Tunisia". **JOAN** *is trying to get* **THOMAS** *[we met him earlier – trying to type] to dance. She follows the rhythm – he just raises a hand and sort swings it about.)*

JOAN. Just follow me – oh come on you look like a statue or something!

THOMAS. Reckon I got two left feet. And my shoelaces are tied together. Look!

> (**JOAN** *laughs.*)

JOAN. Come on just do what I do.

> *(He tries – it's disastrous.)*

THOMAS. *(Whispering.)* Can't we just chat or something?

JOAN. *(Laughing.)* No. No. Try – move your hips – not your feet. And arms up – like this. Oh that's good...

> *(It's not, but* **THOMAS** *so wants to dance for* **JOAN**.*)*

JOAN. And here's the change...

> *(The rhythm change makes them both laugh.* **NYE** *appears in a tie, waistcoat, and a woman's apron, carrying a frying pan.)*

---

* A licence to produce *THE PROMISE* does not include a performance license for any third-party or copyrighted recordings. Licensees should create their own.

NYE. Who wants fried eggs with their ham? Dinner time!

JOAN. More like breakfast – it's four AM! And that's not Spam, is it, Minister?

NYE. Ham'n'eggs. A great American import. Illegal but with friends in high…

> *(He stops because the doorbell goes [it is a string-pulled bell]. Even though the music continues, everyone freezes.)*

JOAN. I'm sober. Like a nun. Shall I go?

NYE. If it's the newspapers, tell them the Minister of Health and Housing is whoring with Paula from Paddington and will call them back when he's finished.

> *(**JOAN** opens the door.)*

(Very surprised.) Ellen?

ELLEN. I was… I saw the lights were on. Nye, I didn't think you'd have guests…

NYE. We were working.

ELLEN. *(Doesn't look like work.)* Oh?

NYE. Let me take your coat. It's still damn cold. Thomas, get Miss Wilkinson some of that whiskey, can you?

> *(**JOAN** lifts the needle off the record player.)*

An American. Charlie Parker, have you heard of him?

ELLEN. I can't say I have – quite a racket.

> *(**THOMAS** hands **ELLEN** a whiskey.)*

So this is 'work'?

NYE. Yes. That young man is the future of architecture, remember the name: Mr Thomas Merrifield…

THOMAS. Sorry but it's Merryman.

> *(Laughter.)*

Though I don't actually mind, Mr Bevan!

NYE. Thomas is a student architect, isn't that so? We are plotting.

ELLEN. Plotting what? I was at the BBC. Broadcasting. How did it get so late? My taxi driver, I swear, was the boatman in a former life, taking us mortals across the river Styx. But Chelsea, and this house, drew me: like a moth, to the lights. Where is Jennie?

> *(**NYE** levels with **ELLEN**.)*

NYE. You have come to interrogate why I didn't stand up for Clem. Yes?

ELLEN. I did come to talk to you about the government – about what is happening.

> *(**NYE** walks off with the plates. The guests are uneasy.)*

Nye, listen to me...

NYE. *(Over his shoulder.)* Alongside that contraband American bourbon – which I got from a contact in the Three Hundred and Ten out of their PX – do you fancy ham and eggs?

ELLEN. Three years ago, you were so principled. "So long as you didn't get lost, Ellen"? Was that it? PRINCIPLES. "Too socialist for the modern Labour Party"? And you were angry then.

NYE. *(Returning.)* I still am. I am still an insurgent. A barbarian, in Mr Morrison's mind.

ELLEN. Joan, is it true he changes his suits at Cardiff Station so that he look less 'well to do' to his constituents in Ebbw Vale?

NYE. *(It is true.)* Of course I do not.

ELLEN. You have given in to the consultants! You are going to let them keep their private practices. The very thing you warned against. You have left them their empires. They will create a system that works for *them*.

NYE. The country will have a National Health Service. It may not be perfect, but it will serve everyone at the point of need.

ELLEN. *(Louder.)* Until the strain gets too much. Things will change, Nye. Costs will go up. Not every government will be as enlightened as you! The Tories will flog it off. It will become national treasure. Up for sale. It will be vulnerable unless it is properly done.

NYE. It is being properly done.

ELLEN. You've left the teaching hospitals alone! And Harley Street! You were going to integrate the pharmaceutical industry and stop their profiteering. That would have reduced costs – but *you* blinked, Minister, you blinked.

> (**JENNIE** *has appeared – unnoticed, in her dressing gown.*)

When Charlie Moran said dance, you forgot who you were.

NYE. That is not true, Ellen.

ELLEN. And you forgot *again* when Ernie asked you if you'd stand against Clem. You forgot, and all you thought about was what would get me, NYE BEVAN, further!

JENNIE. Ellen. It's very late.

> (**ELLEN** *turns – surprised by* **JENNIE**.*)*

ELLEN. Jennie! I woke you, I'm sorry. I am here to report that the good Minister of Health and Housing is distracted. Wallowing in political ambition.

NYE. *(Furious.)* I am not, Ellen. I am not. This is nonsense.

JOAN. I should go, really, Miss Lee, Mr Bevan...

ELLEN. *(Laughing.)* Oh, don't run away! Back in the good old days we'd argue politics until well after the milkman had done his rounds.

JOAN. *(Making light.)* My bike knows its way back to my room in Stockwell. Thomas...?

(**ELLEN** *snaps – surprising everyone.*)

ELLEN. Don't go! No.

JENNIE. Ellen, please. You are tired. We are exhausted.

ELLEN. Jennie – I bet Nye hasn't told you!

JENNIE. You and Herbert plotted and mo...

ELLEN. *(Interrupting.)* We wanted a change of leader yes, indeed we did, BEFORE.

JENNIE. That's not what I am talking about. And you know it.

ELLEN. *(Shocked.)* Jennie?

JENNIE. *(Gently.)* It's very late. Please – get off home...

ELLEN. You mean Herbert and I? That was nothing. Nothing.

JENNIE. *(Stopping her.)* You've been poorly. Come on.

ELLEN. *(Laughing, defensive.)* I'm fine. We cannot stop – we never stopped during the war. Joan, listen to me. Don't turn away. You and Thomas are young. You must look forward. Isn't that so? At my glorious age, which is terminal, by any reckoning, we can only look back. Jennie, I am not poorly – I am dying, I have it on good authority.

NYE. Ellen you are not dying: you just need a long weekend in the country, but who of us doesn't? I want to show you what we have been working on...

JENNIE. Ellen, what do you mean 'dying'?

ELLEN. I don't mean anything Jennie. Nothing. I'm sorry.

JENNIE. Well I have a Select Committee at eight. I think everyone should finish their drinks. We are well past last orders. It's nearly dawn, now please...

ELLEN. You – Miss Vincent – I was once you. An outsider. A woman on a mission. To break through. There were only three women in the House, when I got there. My life – whatever it was going to be, was laid out and waiting for the whole glorious adventure. And Mr Merriman, is it? Handsome fella, Joan, he'll be quite a catch.

JENNIE. Leave Joan be: you are feeling maudlin...

ELLEN. I'm not maudlin, Jennie, this is not some *(Something you can fix.)* ...

(She stops herself – downs her whiskey.)

NYE. Ellen, there's the rank in Eaton Square, I am going to go and fetch you a taxi. Now please...

JOAN. I can help you, Miss Wilkinson, you really should be home...

THOMAS. Mr Bevan, I will make those changes you requested tomorrow, I'll have them done first thing...

ELLEN. *(Hard.)* What do you know of me, Joan really? I mean really.

JOAN. Me...?

ELLEN. Yes – yes. You.

JOAN. Oh everything – you campaigned: for justice. The Jarrow marchers. In parliament. The war. You were famous in Deptford: Dad and Mum would listen to you on the wireless in the war. I'd sit on the stairs. You were so brave. And we always believed in Labour, of course.

JENNIE. Ellen, come on. Let's stop now. Let's all stop.

    (**JENNIE** *goes to* **ELLEN** *and takes her hand.*)

ELLEN. I can't stop, don't you see, I can't Jennie. I can't. I can't sleep, I can't breathe. There is a panther chasing me, creeping behind me. It will pounce soon enough. I can't bear the wait, you see, the dread.

JENNIE. Come on enough. Let's stop this now. You are shivering. Ellen...

ELLEN. *(Breaking from* **JENNIE**.*)* Listen to me, Joan - please.

JENNIE. Will you let her be. Let the lass be.

ELLEN. Did you hear about my glider crash, Joan? I was Minister of Shelters! I'd ended up three thousand feet up in the air looking down at what was left of Portsmouth when the Wing Commander next to me whispered – "We are going to crash" and so we did. Why I've limped ever since. Is there any more of that whiskey, Comrade Bevan? I wasn't brave – I am not brave, Miss Vincent. Deptford, you say?

    (**JOAN** *nods.*)

As the Mistress of Fucking Air Raid Shelters I was sent to places that had been bombed.Not photogenic bombings like Mr Churchill or the King showed up for. These were places where hell had come from the sky. I would toddle along in my little car: me, a driver and a civil servant. Showing the flag: "Whitehall hasn't forgotten you."

    (**JOAN** *turns away.*)

Joan, will you please listen to me! I want you to know this. When you think of me...

JENNIE. Ellen – this is not the right time. I want you to stop this.

ELLEN. *(To* **JOAN** *and* **THOMAS**.*)* That particular morning. A young girl was in the playground. She was practising for a skipping contest, they said.

NYE. Ellen, no, no, it's a long time ago…

ELLEN. She was seven, Nye! She thought 'it' was one of ours and waved. Having cut the little girl in half with his guns, the German then dropped a 1,000 pound bomb straight through the school. The children were having their lunch.

> *(Slight pause.)*

When we arrived – from Whitehall – that afternoon, they were still holding back mothers with grief boiling their innards like they'd swallowed acid. A woman turned to me…

> *(***ELLEN*** *gasps – taps her chest.)*

I can't seem to breathe.

JENNIE. Ellen, have some water. Come along now, and let be. Nye can you…

NYE. Yes, Thomas, could you take Joan to the kitchen, please…

> *(***ELLEN*** *spins – she's gasping now, but powerful, angry and demanding.* ***JOAN*** *is ashen – breathing hard.)*

> *(***ELLEN*** *gasping – scrabbles in her bag.)*

ELLEN. No, no, they have to hear this. A teacher was screaming: "Miss Wilkinson – what will you say *now*? What are you going to tell us now?"

> *(***ELLEN*** *finds her nebuliser – pulls on it.)*

But I had nothing to say. No nonsense about defeating Hitler *whatever* the cost, no Mr Churchill…

(**JOAN** *suddenly runs off, retching,* **THOMAS** *goes after her.*)

THOMAS. Joan…!

(*We hear* **JOAN** *vomiting.*)

ELLEN. Dear God, has the poor girl drunk too much? She's very young Nye.

JENNIE. No, Ellen. Listen to me *now*: her family were killed by a flying bomb. Her father, mother, baby brother. The little boy was five or six. Joan had gone to the chemist as the boy was ill with tonsillitis. She returned to…I think what you described. Excuse me.

(*She follows* **JOAN** *off.* **ELLEN** *is horrified.*)

ELLEN. You should have stopped me Nye. Oh God, I am sorry. I am sorry. I should talk with her…

NYE. Leave be. Ellen, you've always been unstoppable. Joan is very committed to Number 10. She's a remarkable young woman. Her father was a stoker – he wanted everything for her.

ELLEN. (*Remembering her father.*) Her father…

NYE. She idolises you, Ellen. Young Thomas lives in passionate hope of something more between them. We think Joan finds it easy here. She will be alright. Ellen, we will change things.

> (**ELLEN** *sits, exhausted.* **NYE** *takes the cloth off the table, revealing a balsa wood and card model of the 'Bevan House' [only a few were built, ultimately].* **NYE** *then plugs a power cable in. The house lights up from inside. It is very beautiful.*)

Thomas has been helping me. He made this. As Minister of Health and Housing we are designing houses that will make for healthier, happier, lives. Come and look at it, Ellen.

ELLEN. It's rather beautiful.

> (*But she doesn't move.* **JOAN**, **THOMAS** *and* **JENNIE** *return. Now* **ELLEN** *stands.*)

I'm sorry, Joan, I am sorry.

JOAN. I think I may have drunk too much Miss Wilkinson.

> (*She hadn't, everyone's focus goes back to the house.*)

Isn't this something? What Mr Bevan is planning? Tom's model is wonderful, isn't it?

ELLEN. I should have thought – I never meant, Joan, please.

THOMAS. Look, there are no 'out houses', or backs. These homes will have toilets upstairs and down.

NYE. We are going to build thousands. Tens of thousands. Many, many more, hopefully. Look at this. A lavatory and wash basin off the main hall. So when the man returns from work he can wash up – before he joins the family. No more coal dust everywhere.

JOAN. Dad's clothes, his hands, were always filthy from work.

THOMAS. (*He points at a detail.*) Your dad could have changed his clothes when he got back from the docks. Washed up, here, Joan...look...

JENNIE. And look a kitchen, here, big enough for everyone to be together. So when the children are doing their homework they can be supervised by mother as she prepares the evening meal.

> (**THOMAS** *takes* **JOAN***'s hand.*)

NYE. (*Bending into the model.*) Look at the number of windows, Ellen – light, air, ventilation.

JENNIE. No more damp, or mould. In a few years' time – your chest, Ellen, will be a thing of the past.

(**JENNIE***'s hand is on* **NYE***'s shoulder.*)

NYE. We've been doing this night after night. Planning every last detail. Health, housing, education...

ELLEN. And you can build these?

NYE. We will build millions, yes. We are not failing. We won't fail. The future will be what we make it. Not just a health service and housing and good schools but a proud nation. People will look at us, from all over the world, and wonder at what we did. They will wonder about what a country we have made. A new Jerusalem.

ELLEN. *(A whisper.)* But not for me. Not for me.

JOAN. Miss Wilkinson?

(*Thump-thump-thump begins again.*)

PORTER. *(Distant, offstage.)* Miss, miss!

Scene Fourteen

(Dolphin Square.)

(Snow swirls. **ELLEN** *is in her kimono on the floor as the set opens up to a scene of winter Britain – trees and fields.)*

ELLEN. Let me be, please.

(A figure appears out of the snow. He is shrouded in cigar smoke; **ELLEN** *stares at him.)*

Winston? What are you doing here?

*(***WINSTON CHURCHILL*** *doesn't answer but pulls on his cigar.* **ELLEN** *has pills and wine. She takes pills, drinks the wine.)*

I can't sleep.

(She takes some more pills.)

These little blighters – they don't half take the edge off things. I CANNOT SLEEP.

WINSTON. Neither can I! Never. Not ever. Pacing, pacing all night. Not a peep. My dear, it is freezing in here – all the windows are open...

ELLEN. Why are you in my room?

WINSTON. *Your* room? I have no idea!

(The thump-thump-thump.)

JOAN. *(Distant, offstage.)* Miss Wilkinson. Miss Wilkinson.

ELLEN. That girl worshipped me, she reminded me of me. The intensity.

WINSTON. Girl, what girl?

*(***ELLEN*** *stares at* **WINSTON**, *the thump-thump-thump.)*

ELLEN. What's that terrible noise?

WINSTON. I have a suspicion that that, my dear, is my gun carriage thumping along the cobbles up to St Paul's. And I am in my coffin. Carried in. The great cathedral dome above me.

> *(He laughs, a new idea.)*

Or maybe – dear Lord – it's the clods of earth landing on your coffin?

ELLEN. I'm frightened.

WINSTON. What of?

ELLEN. I don't want to die.

WINSTON. *(The pills and the wine on the floor.)* By the look of things, my dear, you may have chased that particular horse from its stable, and it is bounding around the paddock. Why did you do that?

> *(**ELLEN** moans and shivers.)*

ELLEN. I am finished. Too knackered…

WINSTON. You could have surrendered. I'd have so enjoyed your memoirs. Long lunches. I'm sure there would have been hundreds of dreary functions.

ELLEN. Switzerland, even.

WINSTON. *(Laughing.)* Ah now that really *would* explain the pills and the vino!

> *(A **YOUNG BOY** starts to sing – "Jerusalem".)*

YOUNG BOY.	WINSTON. *(During.)*
AND DID THOSE FEET IN ANCIENT TIME WALK UPON ENGLAND'S MOUNTAINS GREEN?	What a lovely voice!

AND WAS THE HOLY LAMB OF GOD ON ENGLAND'S PLEASANT PASTURES SEEN?

AND DID THE COUNTENANCE DIVINE SHINE FORTH UPON OUR CLOUDED HILLS?

AND WAS JERUSALEM BUILDED HERE AMONG THOSE DARK SATANIC MILLS?

WINSTON. Do you know, the boy is singing about your Jerusalem! Ellen, your Jerusalem!

ELLEN. I don't have a Jerusalem...

WINSTON. What a beautiful thing you all dream of!

ELLEN. It's not a dream...

WINSTON. Oh come on! Every man – whatever his standing – doffing his oily cap, raising his trilby, or leaning down from his Bentley – all 'equal' amongst the rolling green of England. Mr Bevan's dark and filthy mines tamed. They are suddenly beacons of humanity, places filled with noble workers breaking coal to power this nation while dear Mr Attlee bowls his googlies to decent working-class lads, cheering them on to a better chance in their pitiful lives. That's your Jerusalem!

(Rising to his theme.)

Or – or – or honest fishermen setting off from the Northumberland coast; farmers bravely astride their tractors hailing the sun-rise, grinning like clowns, or noble fellas in the Caribbean, or cotton pickers in Rajasthan all happy in the service of *your* Jerusalem. But then, just so our spirits are all free to fly, somewhere back in the old country, in a fragrant vale – of gorse and heather – your Miss Lee has requisitioned a country house to give THE people their first taste of poetry. You are all so bloody worthy.

(He laughs.)

WINSTON. But all of this must be *elsewhere*. It must be *away* from furnaces making iron and steel. Away from ships being built plate by welded plate. Away from the real mines. The filth, the violence of work. The shit. There is nothing noble. It is the shocking iniquity of 'capital' versus labour!

ELLEN. For God's sake, Winston, go away. I want to sleep.

WINSTON. Until YOU have built Jerusalem!

ELLEN. Please...

> *(She starts to crawl. He follows her, his feet thump-thump. The singing gets louder.)*

WINSTON. Until you have rid everyone of pain and fear! But that is not how we are, Ellen. You *know* it's not how we are. Of course, we have absolute power to build this great cathedral but also power to destroy everything. Have you seen what we did to defeat the Japanese? Infamy. And you fret about schools, or milk for growing bones, or hospitals, or houses with indoor shitters, all in the quaint certainty that every day you can make lives – pitiful lives – better. A step closer to your Jerusalem.

> *(His voice now echoes around the theatre.)*

But I've seen it all and I know. I know. And damn it Ellen – you know, too.

We humans are messy and frightened, and we betray each other and kill to survive, or just because we can! Faith? Phooey. Equality? Why on God's earth? Some are born to lead, some to serve. It's simple, and it's essential. Everything you have wanted – everything goes against God's order. Life is cruel. People are cruel. You know that, you of all people know that. Your order is no different from Stalin's or Hitler's. You have a dream, and you want to thrust it down people's throats.

Come on, dear Ellen. Let go – you *know*. You *know* people just want to be free: free to live, free to rut like animals, free to be saints, free to die. We are so grubby and cruel. Your Jerusalem!

(**ELLEN** *pulls herself up or tries to.*)

ELLEN. No, Winston, no. There is more. There is more...

(*The thump thump thump is now cacophonous against the singing and* **WINSTON***'s voice.*)

WINSTON. They have come for you, Ellen. Come to take you home.

PORTER. *(Calling.)* Miss, Miss, you alright?

WINSTON. Come to take you home.

JOAN. *(Shouting, offstage.)* Miss – open up. We are here! Open up.

WINSTON. They have come to take you home!

(**WINSTON** *is gone in a cloud of cigar smoke.* **ELLEN** *rises slightly.*)

ELLEN. Quiet – please. Let's please be quiet. Shh everyone. Quiet. Everyone, please. Quiet. Quiet.

(*She slumps. Foetal. Finally, the door opens.* **JOAN** *with the* **PORTERS** *behind her, stares at* **ELLEN***'s body.*)

Scene Fifteen

(The garden, 10 Downing Street.)

*(**ELLEN**'s body remains. **CLEM** is in his dressing gown. **VIOLET** appears in her night clothes.)*

CLEM. Listen. It's started to thaw.

(Pause.)

I like to listen to London waking up. The Horse Guards have started again. Telegraph boys. Adventurous souls on their way home to bed.

VIOLET. Clem you will exhaust yourself. Please.

(A doorbell tinkles somewhere in the house.)

It's very early.

*(**ERNIE** appears in his coat; he is pale and tired.)*

ERNIE. Clem, a word?

*(**ERNIE** is reluctant to speak.)*

VIOLET. It's five thirty in the morning. If the Russians are invading, the sooner we all know, the better.

ERNIE. Prime Minister?

*(**CLEM** nods to **ERNIE**.)*

Ellen's dead.

VIOLET. *(Deeply shocked.)* Oh no. No.

ERNIE. An associate I have at Scotland Yard contacted me.

(This is huge.)

They think she may have taken her own life. Her pills.

VIOLET. The bloody fool. No.

ERNIE. *(Thinking ahead.)* Herbert is in hospital, Clem. His heart...

CLEM. He must be told. They were great colleagues. We need to manage this very carefully.

VIOLET. What is the matter with you?

> *(**CLEM** looks at her – surprised. **ERNIE** looks away.)*

CLEM. Something terrible has happened...

VIOLET. Yes. Ellen has killed herself.

CLEM. *May* have killed herself. That is the last we talk like that.

> *(**ERNIE** is now very uncomfortable.)*

I'm sorry, Ernie.

ERNIE. Not this morning, Clem, I am going.

CLEM. *(Steel, stopping him.)* No, listen to me.

> *(Slight pause.)*

Will you do a broadcast, Ernie? About Ellen. Would you do that? She must not be forgotten.

> *(**ERNIE** can't speak. He nods and goes. **VIOLET** and **CLEM** are alone. They are further apart than they have ever been.)*

Vi', dear, rustle us up some tea, don't you think? It's suddenly rather chilly.

> *(**VIOLET** doesn't move.)*

We must carry on.

> *(He turns to **VIOLET** but she doesn't look at him.)*

CLEM. We must go on. For the people. We serve the people.

> (**CLEM** *pulls out his pipe and walks purposefully back into Number 10.* **VIOLET** *remains.* **ELLEN** *is dead, buried in snow.)*

End

AT THE POINT
OF NEED

AT THE POINT OF NEED was first performed at the Old Vic Theatre in 2018 as part of The Greatest Wealth – In Celebration of the NHS. The performance starred David Threlfall and was directed by Adrian Lester.

(He is white, working class, middle-aged, not in great shape. He has an engaging laugh. He stands alone onstage. He wears a black suit, white shirt, dark tie. This is the suit he will be buried in.)

HIM. It's warm. Thump. Whoosh. Thump. Suddenly everything is urgent. Pressure, colour, light. Green cloth. And now I am gulping. Gasping. Now, hot flesh. What I'll learn is a smile.

White enamelled tin, hard, towel, a blanket. Him holding me. Smell of tobacco.

Home. The little fire. They don't have much. For me they have everything and more!

Wow that hurts! Brushed steel, a tiny cloud of cotton wool, the stinging... but we lads are brave.

Crates of milk, peeling the tops back, drinking, loving, but wretchin' also.

Teacher has hair on her chin. Luke's arms aren't there: just fingers wriggling like worms. We stare at him. Sometimes someone makes a joke. But mostly we just look away.

"Nineteen sixty!" he says, "Who'd 'ave effing thought it." And I am sent to bed and there's laughing downstairs.

Father has it behind his back. She says – "Six years old, little man." Her eyes are hot, and proud. I run and take the shiny bike.

He holds the seat and starting with a walk, now running, making sure I stay straight. "Stay straight!"

Waiting for the doc', I ask her about the boy with the rusty red hair. Moulded to his front is a yellow tin with a slot and on his legs are moulded callipers. I am staring at the plastic statue. "What's a calliper?" I ask to stop thinking about how very very terrible my pain is, and the blood running down my leg. "You won't need to worry, children don't get polio any more."

She smiles. I love Mum.

Father has some squash. Wants a word... How would I like a brother or a sister?

He is right. Everything changes. Mum is tired.

She is kneeling in the khazi, her back retching. She pushes the door shut.

He says "leave-well-alone" and winks. She's gone and Nan comes and Father and me – we-do-what-we-are told!

The hospital. Rows of beds, women, people, kids like me, visiting. Nurses, flowers. Faces smiling.

The baby is noisy – things do change! I am breaking some flower pots in the garden. "You want to leave my pots alone, sunny Jim." I didn't know Dad was watching and feel bad.

We four go to the sea-side. Sister and I sleep in bunks and Father and Mother share up front in the caravan. The sun burns the glass and the metal around it in the morning.

With some boys I play war. We have a tin helmet. The real McCoy. I get hit by a brick – a stick grenade – and the next thing I know is my eye is swollen. Father tells the nurse "It's real shiner." But as a precaution, I stay in for the night. It's dark – just light down the ward and I am bein' sick. It's all over the sheet.

"What's wrong soldier?" A different nurse comes out of the dark. I'm embarrassed. I am ten and should be able...but my head hurts and I am frightened and ask if I have polio like the boy with the calliper. She puts the hard glass of the thermometer under my tongue.

Measles. Isolation.

Their uniforms are crisp, they smile at me and I love the toast they have. Once a girl stops and stares through the doorway. I wave.

Father comes when others visit and brings a Commando comic. As he is going, he smiles: "You're good with people, son. Make friends, easily. That's something to treasure."

Nan is a bit wobbly on her feet and I go when I can after football. The top of her hands are blue and her nails silvery. I show her *Melody Maker*, she chats about the telly, the strikes, the Irish.

One afternoon she is sitting on the floor in her kitchen. I say: "Shall we go to the doctor, nan?"

They send an ambulance. I try and help pick her up but they say "We are Professionals." The tall one said I did the right thing to call and shakes my fucking hand!

My face looks like Vesuvius. But my hair is OK. Dad teases: "Feels like I am living with four women! All this flippin' shampoo." I like music – ELP, stuff like that. Jethro Tull. I don't care if that makes me a weirdo.

I go to see Nan in hospital. I reckon she is dead, then she winks at me and I nearly piss myself. Happy.

At her funeral, Mother is crying and shuddering. All I can think is there's been a mistake – my mind isn't really focussed.

It's raining cats and dogs. Mum and Dad sit up front. I am squeezed in the back amongst all my stuff.

"You are the first" Dad is saying, and I notice him turn away sort of shy. "He'll make friends, he's good with people." Mum is crying. He puts his hand on her as they go back to the car, and I feel alone.

Freshers week. I keep myself to myself. Man of mystery. But I'm good with people, make friends, girl-friends. One or three...

> *(He laughs.)*

Fuck me this is *not* good. So. I am at the Casualty in town knowing I have fucked my life up. Geddit?

> *(He laughs.)*

After five hours and a few smokes and a Marathon Bar a nurse takes me to a cubicle. I love the NHS. She's seen a nervous student before, I'd reckon. "Why are you here, love?" And I tell her about the fucking agonising pain when I piss. "Mind if we have a look"

(Horrified.) A look! Oh fuck never really thought this through. A look! "I can't understand what you are saying Mum!?"

Sally: "Father collapsed in the garden near the shed" ... near where I broke the pots. "I'll come home" I say and I know DAD will be there, waiting for me: laughing at my hair, and knowin' – the way he catches my eye – that he understands who it is to be me.

But I am falling out of a plane. Don't know when I will hit the ground.

I can't breathe my ears are ringing. "They are fucking amazing..." I shout "What?" She smiles and turns away from me. So, we are smoking outside – it's too hot in there. The band is turned up to eleven.

Di'.

They say nothing is perfect but we are pressed into each other on my bed. This *is* perfect.

One photos shows it all. Her, me, Mum, the sisters, Barry and a few others. Smiling. Di' and me. Grinning.

"Push now, dear."

Di' is cursing: fuck you, fuck this, shit and fuck but the Professionals have done it all before. That here 'it' comes. And here it is. And all the joy and relief and confusion wrapped in a white towel. NHS embroidered on one side.

We call her Sophie. Di' has brought class to my clan. Sophie, then Annie.

I'm a father and a man who supports a football team, a man who works nine to five selling cars, a man who has a mortgage, a man who worries more than he shows. A man who loves his girls.

Things *change*, don't they, between men and women?

The goon at the Travelodge reception teases us: we shouldn't be there at the three in the afternoon.

I am more nervous than I can remember. I'm praying she won't come out of the loo but the door lock clicks. She lies beside me. Her belly is scarred, she says, as I pull at the lace she is wearing and we both blush.

This is *my* life. This is *her* life. Mrs Browning, from accounts. It has been coming, it has been brewing. The soft light of the Travelodge makes her skin soft and grey, me hairy, my skin pink, bruised looking.

Di' doesn't know, or notice, a thing. Does she care? Her mind is on other things. Work, the girls. She's taken up dancing.

But she is telling me something.

"I'm not sure I'm very well. I went to see Dr Verma, at the practice." One of the girls is upstairs and so I say "Keep your voice down."

We wait. The place is heaving. Some people look fine, some have lost all their hair.

Did me with Mrs Browning bring us *here*? Was it Dad dying how he did? Sudden. Or is it just how life changes...

I take Di's hand. "You OK?" I remember how we once were. How we hung onto each other to stop falling out of bed. How it was perfect.

The Consultant is gentle – but hard to hear.

Di' puts up a fight and Mrs Browning and I stop. I can't lie: like something really unfair has taken away our afternoons. Di' is dying and I can't, we can't...

(Horrified.) What am I? What am I saying?

The nurses are amazing! "Di' – dear – the vomiting will stop." A nurse says rubbing her back like I no longer seem able to do. And later when the girls have gone Di' can't hold it in. I run to the Sister at the nurses' station she just looks at me and smiles: "That's OK, Tony. Happens all the time..." She's from Jamaica, and as she walks down the ward I see how everything has changed in the NHS. Men and women in the ward, visitors all the time. The clothes the staff wear have changed. The man mopping the floor.

Di' is dying. I am waiting for the girls to come with Barry. He and Sheila are saints. Di' looks at us all – and she smiles. She smiles that it is okay, like Di' always tries to make it. It is okay. It's okay. And we kiss.

I never go back to the Travelodge.

I sleep in the bed I shared with Di' for twenty-four years. Her things are still on the dressing table and her smalls in the drawers. I take them out at night. Smell washing powder, hard cotton, even a bit of lace. And I miss her.

The girls absorb everything but home becomes something where they once were. I dream of Di'. But it gets less...

So-and-so to room ten, so-and-so to the phlebotomist. Dr Verma left when Virgin took the surgery on. It runs like clockwork now.

You're Irish, or Scottish, I say to Dr Grazfeld, laughing. I'm good with people. No, she says, from Germany.

"You need to lose some weight." Tell that to my tailor – runs through my head but I am sweating a bit. I smile, but words Sophie said to me last night when she came over with Erik are hot in my head. "You ignored Mum's symptoms!" "She never *said* there was anything wrong." I am shouting and Sophie is crying and Erik says it's time they went.

I tell him he is a sanctimonious cunt. Then I see Sophie's eyes. "Please" I want to say "I never meant this to happen. I meant..."

Dr Grazfeld is on about diabetes. Of course she's a Kraut. "Will you stay now?" I grin friendly but I'm angry still about last night with Sophie and Erik. About everything. "We couldn't have gone on like we were!" I'm into something now. Too many people everywhere. It's not personal. She's not interested.

I sell the house. It has made more than I earnt. Catchment area. Good for schools.

I ask Annie to tell her sister to come and collect her things but Sophie and Erik, and the little girl, never come.

"What are you doing at Christmas?" Mrs Browning and I are in the car park. "I'll pop into see my mother" I say "She's not really with us now." But she touches my hand: "Come to ours. The kids are coming. Gordon is cooking so I'll need company. And no-one should be alone..."

Gordon and *Delyth* Browning are kind to each other and we all have a happy day. There's talk about the Coding, but no-one seems troubled. Gordon reckons "It's the only way."

At the front door I want to say something to him about the Travelodge, so as not to lie, but just thank him and give her a kiss on the cheek. Delyth – there's none of the heat from our Thursdays. That was fifteen years ago.

(He sits.)

Annie is at the door. She is the spitting image of her mother – she's older than Di' when she died. I look up at her from my chair. She asks: "Has no-one been in?"

I have been home now two – maybe three – months and no, no-one's been in. Annie bustles around. Tidying, loading the dishwasher. I am embarrassed.

I've felt so odd. I keep looking down. One foot – not two.

"You'll feel it, like a foreign country" – the surgeon had said. They have no time in the Public Hospitals – and certainly she had no time. "I am frightened they'd lop the wrong one off" I said, laughing up at the orderly on our way to the op'. He didn't look at me. Not once.

"How are your children? I've not seen them for a while." "Not children anymore" Annie says and she turns away busy cleaning but I can see that she is crying. "They *should* help you Dad, someone should help you." I try and sound like it's the best thing in the world and say, to stop her tears. "Oh, that all went years ago. I'm OK." She works like a demon. Clearing, cleaning...

"How is Sophie? Do you two still see each other?" Annie nods – they do. "That is good." I think. "Tell her..." But I stop myself. You can never go back, only forward.

Nearly seventy! In a chair. Living in a sweat suit.

The girls have moved on. They must now be... I'm forgetting dates, numbers. I look for Sophie on Friendsbook. I find her. She's smiling. No Erik, anywhere. He wasn't right for Sophie.

Today, the Time-Feed says, is my birthday. I don't press the Memories tab. No! Need a bevvy, not memories.

It has started to rain but sod it Tony we need to raise a glass, maybe meet some people. We are good with people.

The car was adapted but it leaks. It's old. I lost the foot now nearly twenty years ago.

> *(He laughs.)*

It starts first time! There is a God! Two lads slide by on those HoverLiners. They are grinning, but I can't see their eyes.

When I get to The Stag and Hunter – get to where I *know* the fucking things is – NOTHING.

Just a gap and the rain. A bevvy, I need a bevvy. It's my birthday. Where do people go now, I wonder?

The Hub. Underground is full of cars. All charging. Over there – Lifts to shops and eateries, Experi-zones. We're okay here.

> *(Slight pause.)*

My chair is behind the seat, I pull it out and heave myself across. Christ I've put on some weight.

> *(Laughing.)*

I am on the ground. I missed the sodding chair. People walk past. "Can you help me?" "Excuse me..." but they go on – there's a moving walkway. I'm a stranger, I suppose.

The first thing I see is their boots. My heart is beating so hard my ears ring.

"Hello, there." He looks down at me, smiles. The other stands back. "I'm stuck. Fell out of my car. Can you, lads...? "But he steps forward, takes my hand – he is wearing plastic gloves – and the bugger runs a Coder across my wrist!

"Seventy-four today, Tony!" He reads off his Code-grab, laughs "You trying to make trouble?" "Looking to have a drink, buddy" I say. Good with people, I smile.

The second laughs "Look at the state of you!" He looks at his scanner, glances to the other man.

A woman looks, then scurries away.

First one whispers: "Cummon, we'd better get you cleared up..."

I'm cold. I've been lying here for ten minutes. "Guys, *just* give me a hand up..." I say trying to sound like it is the easiest thing in the world but *the* code. The code. Dr Grazfeld gave it me. We all have it.

"We'll sort the car", the men say, and put me in their van easy, nice as pie. I say through the cage. "Just drop me off home, lads." It is still raining. I turn to the cage again "I'm a diabetic, I need my pad..." "We know, Tony. They'll have everything." Then, to the guy driving: "There she is!"

Just a flash as she runs past the window. Bang bang – the doors go, my two guys are out. I hear: "Oh come on Mrs Kitari, don't be a douche." I feel sick now – hungry, thirsty.

"Without an account we are going to process you through Public Accounts, do you understand, Mr Foster" I am lying flat. My back hurts like fuck. "Why didn't you get an account?" She says more in sorrow than in anger. "Is there anyone you know who has an account? Your daughters?"

I blink. A few angry words – it was bad time, I was a fool. I know that.

Nope. Nope. Nope. "Can you sign that you understand what it means to be Public Accounts" and she holds a E-Pad over me.

The woman, Mrs Kitari, is next to me as we go in. She's younger and she's crying.

They take my wheelies. I am sitting on a leatherette chair. There are hundreds of other chairs in lines. "I'm Tony" I say to Mrs Kitari, with a smile. Her eyes are so beautiful.

One of the Public Accounts people takes two children on leads to a table. Everyone is smiling.

"Was my birthday. I went out to get a drink. Daft fuck. Wrong turning and here I am. What about you?" I whisper, trying to laugh, keep it light.

"I was very hungry" she leans across "I was begging. BEGGING. And someone reported me as a nuisance."

I whisper: "We should stick together, you and me, Mrs Kitari." I like her. A bell rings. We stop, just look ahead.

The food is not terrible. We sleep in dormitories. With the prostate I need a rubber thingy at beddy byes... the less said the better.

The scale is enormous and whoever runs Public Account Twenty-Nine is onto a nice earner. Everything is efficient. Including what happens when people pass.

After Father in the garden, then Di', then Mother, I watch people passing like one of those guys in the Pacific in the Second War. The sharks circle. There's a scream and...

I suppose they had to do something: people were dying in the street, or alone, at home.

Sometimes at night I think of it all. How we used to... I think...have a system. Those little third of a pint bottles of milk at school. The inoculations. The GP who knew my name...

(He laughs.)

The hospitals. The care for Di'.

Right through her chemo no-one ever asked if she had insurance. But it changed. I needed help after she went, after Sophie and that row. I was lost. We all fail, sometimes, don't we?

(Slight pause.)

"Gym, me?!" I'm giggling with Mrs Kitarai. I liked a bevvy too much and sin of sins, I smoked. I tell her how I smoked with Mrs Browning in the Travelodge waiting for the blue pill to wear down... "Can't walk out with that in your pocket!" She'd laugh.

But was I worse than anyone else?

(He shrugs.)

I tell Mrs Kitari these things. She tells me what happened to her. It's what we are left with. Our story.

Today, I don't know where Mrs Kitari has got to. Someone said she had to join a Workgroup.

I just hope the sharks didn't get her.

(Lights fade. Blackness.)

Milton Keynes UK
Ingram Content Group UK Ltd.
UKHW050123180724
445629UK00010B/102

9 780573 000614